Spiritual Profiling is really about understanding that we have different kinds of neighbors we are called to love and engage. Pastor Hovestol takes us through the different types of people who inhabited Jesus' world and how He interacted with them as a way to help us with the different kinds of people we meet. The study is solid and intriguing. It will lead us to consider how to relate well to the variety of people around us; a profitable study, well worth the time.

—**Dr. Darrell Bock**
   Professor of New Testament Studies at
   Dallas Theological Seminary and
   New York Times bestselling author

Pastor Tom Hovestol's very readable work draws attention to a reality of life that Christians commonly overlook as they consider ministry to others. By means of copious references to the Scriptures (specifically, to the examples provided by the Lord Jesus Himself), the author provides insights and appropriate instruction for how Christians might show respect for the diversity of viewpoints held by different people. This offers valuable guidance both for those who wish to evangelize wisely and those who want to be salt and light in a 21st century world. The author's style is irenic and respectful, exactly what we would expect from an individual who has spent many hours drinking from the well of Jesus' wisdom.

—**Dr. Ken Bickel**
   Professor of Pastoral Studies
   Grace Theological Seminary

Here is a fresh reading of Jesus' ministry, a creative tutorial developed for every hungry disciple who wants to "recentralize" Christ in their faith. With a pastor's grasp of his time and a prophet's passion for true-hearted devotion, Hovestol helps us critique the " " " own day.

—**Dr. Andrew J. Schmut**
   Professor of Bible
   Moody Bible Institute

In *Spiritual Profiling* Pastor Tom has given us a new lens through which to view ourselves and others. His diligent research into eight religious cultures of Jesus' day forms the basis for a fresh perspective on the expressions of those cultures in our world. The companion online assessment tool brings a sharp and personal focus to the application of these biblical insights. This is a must read for those seeking to genuinely and effectively live out the life of Jesus in our pluralistic society.

—**Stephen LeBar**, PhD
Former Executive Director, CBAmerica

A luminous exposé of the loving wisdom and brilliance of Jesus! There is refreshing and penetrating insight here. This is a much-needed read for the next generation of the church as it engages a globalized and pluralistic world with the gospel.

—**Heath Hardesty**
NextGen Pastor, Valley Community Church

How should you relate today to the unchurched, the dechurched, religious syncretists, do-gooders, traditionalists, and several other groups of people? The answer is found in the surprising ways that Jesus related to these kinds of people in His day. Tom Hovestol has given us the gift of new lenses to see more clearly how Jesus related with diverse groups of people. He has also handed us new tools so that we can relate to similar people just like Jesus did—and always with grace and truth.

—**Brian Mavis**
Executive Director of Externally Focused Network

Clever. Fresh. Insightful. Interesting. Fun. Challenging. *Spiritual Profiling* takes us down a biblical path we have not traveled before. Tom Hovestol combines the discipline of a scholar with the warmth of a pastor to give us a fresh look at Jesus and his relationships.

—**Leith Anderson**
President, National Association of Evangelicals, Washington, D.C.;
Pastor, Wooddale Church, Eden Prairie, MN

TOM HOVESTOL

SPIRITUAL PROFILING

HOW JESUS INTERACTED WITH
8 DIFFERENT TYPES *of* PEOPLE
AND WHY IT MATTERS FOR YOU

MOODY PUBLISHERS
CHICAGO

All Scripture quotations, unless otherwise indicated, are taken from the *Holy Bible, New International Version*®, NIV®. Copyright ©1973, 1978, 1984 by Biblica, Inc.™ Used by permission of Zondervan. All rights reserved worldwide.

Scripture quotations marked KJV are taken from the King James Version.

Edited by Jim Vincent
Interior Design: Ragont Design
Cover Design: Studio Gearbox (www.studiogearbox.com)
Author Photo: Scott Phillips

Library of Congress Cataloging-in-Publication Data

Hovestol, Tom.
    Spiritual profiling : how Jesus interacted with 8 types of people . . . and why it matters for you / Tom Hovestol.
        p. cm.
    Includes bibliographical references.
    ISBN: 978-0-8024-5713-4
    1. Spirituality. 2. Spiritual life—Christianity. 3. Personality—Religious aspects—Christianity. 4. Temperament—Religious aspects—Christianity. I. Title.
    BV4501.3.H6833 2010
    248.2--dc22

                                                            2010019151

We hope you enjoy this book from Moody Publishers. Our goal is to provide high-quality, thought-provoking books and products that connect truth to your real needs and challenges. For more information on other books and products written and produced from a biblical perspective, go to www.moodypublishers.com or write to:

Moody Publishers
820 N. LaSalle Boulevard
Chicago, IL 60610

1 3 5 7 9 10 8 6 4 2

Printed in the United States of America

To my beloved congregation
at Calvary Church in Longmont, Colorado.
Several years ago we adopted a church motto that has
come to characterize us in profound and practical ways:
Broken people, being made new in Jesus,
overflowing with gratitude and poured out for others.
For twenty years we have walked this path of
discipleship together, and I could not be more grateful for
the innumerable ways God has used you for good in my life.

CONTENTS

Introduction: A New Kind of Profiling   9

1. Jesus and the Unchurched   21
   Profile: The Gentiles
2. Jesus and the Detached   47
   Profile: The Detached Jews
3. Jesus and the Syncretists   75
   Profile: The Samaritans
4. Jesus and the Traditionalists   105
   Profile: The Sadducees
5. Let's Meet the Pharisees   135
   An Introduction
6. Jesus and the Do Gooders   147
   Profile: The Hillel Pharisees
7. Jesus and the Truth Seekers   173
   Profile: The Shammai Pharisees
8. Jesus and the Passionate Ones   205
   Profile: The Zealots
9. Jesus and the Super Spiritual   239
   Profile: The Essenes

Conclusion   265
Notes   277
Acknowledgments   287

A NEW KIND *of* PROFILING

"Profiling" is a dirty word, and yet we can't stop doing it. On the one hand, profiling raises the specter of racial prejudice, ethnic cleansing, hate crimes, and putting people into boxes. All of these are evil and should make us feel dirty. On the other hand, profiling can save lives and save time, protect the innocent and more easily apprehend the guilty, develop people, and build better teams. And these contribute to the common good. Let's look at some examples, bad and good, of profiling.

Ethnic profiling has left a legacy of horrendous suffering. It was practiced by the Turks against the Armenians in 1915, the Nazis against the Jews in the 1930s and 40s, the Americans against the Japanese in 1942, and the Hutus against the Tutsis in Rwanda in 1994, to mention only a few examples.

"Driving While Black" (DWB) has become a catch phrase for the evils of racial profiling. DWB refers to a motorist stopped by police officers, questioned, and sometimes searched simply because the driver is black. Based on skin color, a person makes generalized judgments about others. Such generalizations have resulted in horrible miscarriages of justice. A much publicized incident of alleged racial profiling in 2009 involved eminent black Harvard University professor Henry Louis Gates being arrested by local police for breaking and entering a Cambridge, Massachusetts home—his own residence!

The increased threat of terrorism since September 11, 2001 has made airport profiling a necessity. An airline security agent who saw Mohamed Atta, the key figure in the 9/11 terrorist plot, board the airplane that day revealed that he thought when he saw Atta and an accomplice, "If this doesn't look like two Arab terrorists, I've never seen two Arab terrorists."[1] As the threat of terrorism continues and becomes more sophisticated and dangerous, an outcry for more and better profiling is sure to occur.

With the human genome having been mapped, genetic profiling is now available. Medical breakthroughs may be on the horizon benefiting millions of human beings. However, data gathered from genetic profiling may be used to deny insurance coverage or charge more for it. Sometimes information is valuable to know and other times it can be costly.

Psychological profiling has ancient roots and myriad modern fruits. Since the time of Hippocrates those who observe the human personality have realized that people are different, yet they fall into somewhat predictable patterns. A plethora of psychological tests are being used to help us understand ourselves and others better, maximize our strengths, screen for possible problems, and build better teams. But psychological profiling has also been used to place people into boxes, label them, and miss the invaluable uniqueness within.

What about spiritual profiling? Are there discernable patterns of religious belief and behavior? Do people tend to gravitate toward identifiable spiritual expressions, and if so, why and how? Every world religion has its sects and denominations. Would it be helpful to understand how I (and others) work religiously? Any parent knows that his or her children are different and must be dealt with according to their bent. Does God deal differently with people who have different spiritual bents?

These questions set me on a course that has resulted in the book you are about to read. I began with a premise. Though each human being is unique, we share a lot in common. Though each age has its special challenges, we respond similarly. And though people living two thousand years ago in Israel were different than we are, we can, and should, relate to them. Thus, I have always found the life and times of Jesus to hold special allure. And so, reading through the Gospels yet again, I noticed how diverse the cast of characters was with whom Jesus interfaced. And it struck me that He seemed to deal with different people differently. I wondered if there was any pattern to Jesus' interactions.

Immediately I recognized that Jesus' world was far more religiously pluralistic than I imagined. He grew up and headquartered His ministry in "Galilee of the Gentiles." He regularly rubbed shoulders with polytheistic and superstitious Romans, with philosophical and sophisticated Greeks, with hearty-partying pagans and with God-fearing Africans. The Bible tells us that Jesus, unlike His fellow countrymen, did not avoid the despised and syncretistic Samaritans. Nor did Jesus shun the Jews who were considered persona non grata in the local synagogues, like those who worked for the occupying government, or who rejected Hebrew ways in favor of Greek, or who lived hellion lifestyles. Moreover, Jesus interacted with individuals representing all of the major religious sects of Judaism.

So I began to specifically delineate groups of people with whom Jesus interacted. Josephus, the first-century Jewish historian, provided four clear groups: the Sadducees, the Pharisees, the Zealots, and the Essenes. The Mishnah (the record of Jewish oral tradition from the time of Jesus to around AD 200) provided numerous clear distinctions between two groups of Pharisees, the followers of Hillel and the followers of Shammai. Then a simple reading of the New Testament provided three more groups: the Gentiles, the disenfranchised Jews, and the Samaritans.

With these eight groups in mind I decided to read through the Gospels carefully, identifying every incident where Jesus interacted with an individual or a group from each of the spiritual profiles. I wondered, does Jesus treat them all the same, or does Jesus treat these different spiritual profiles differently? Surprisingly I found that Jesus dealt with each group differently, and *consistently*. This piqued my interest.

Is it possible that people tend to fall into specific spiritual profiles? Is it possible that the kinds of people Jesus interacted with are like the kinds of people one would find in any place at any time? Is it possible that the kinds of people Jesus dealt with in His world are parallel to the kinds of people we have in our world today?

So an idea was born. And as I often do, I decided to pursue it with a group of people from my church, Calvary Church in Longmont, Colorado. During Sunday evenings in the summer of 2008, participants learned together about spiritual profiles. Their give-and-take not only helped me define and refine insights gained from the Gospels, but also convinced me that our pursuit of the spiritual profiles was useful.

Let me introduce you to a new kind of profiling, the result of my findings after our students had immersed themselves in the different spiritual profiles with which Jesus interacted. There are eight spiritual profiles, and every religious (or nonreligious) person falls into one of the profiles. Here are the eight, and the overarching question about each:

1. *Jesus and the Unchurched* (the Gentiles). How did Jesus interact with people with a pagan religious background?
2. *Jesus and the Detached* (the detached Jews). How did Jesus interact with those who were disconnected from the religious establishment of the day?
3. *Jesus and the Syncretists* (the Samaritans). How did Jesus interact with those who fused diverse beliefs into a syncretistic spirituality?
4. *Jesus and the Traditionalists* (the Sadducees). How did Jesus interact with those who sought to preserve the ancient words and rituals of the faith?
5. *Jesus and the Do Gooders* (the Pharisees who followed Hillel). How did Jesus interact with those who were known for their passionate pursuit of goodness?

6. *Jesus and the Truth Seekers* (the Pharisees who followed Shammai). How did Jesus interact with those who were intent on rightly dividing the Word of truth?

7. *Jesus and the Passionate Ones* (the Zealots). How did Jesus interact with those whose politics dominated their worldview?

8. *Jesus and the Super Spiritual* (the Essenes). How did Jesus interact with those whose approach to spirituality was inward and communal?

We explored, as you will, (1) the historical background of each spiritual profile, which helped us to see the individuals as real people—like ourselves—and (2) the tendencies of each spiritual profile, in order to identify the basic beliefs and behaviors of each group. The ten components of the tendencies form an acrostic: T*ruth*, E*conomics*, N*eighborhood*, D*evotion*, E*veryman*, N*ature of God*, C*ivics*, I*mmortality*, E*thics*, and S*ummary*. They are the basis of many of our "What Is Your Profile?" assessment questions, which are available online at www.spiritualprofiling.com. We encourage you to answer the assessment questions. They will help you recognize your own profile; those "test" questions, along with the TENDENCIES section, should enable you to start making the connections between yourself and particular spiritual profiles.

The TENDENCIES for each group appear early in each chapter of this book. The bulk of each chapter is entitled "Watch Jesus." This section will present Jesus' interactions with several people representing each spiritual profile. This section should be both profound and practical. It is my hope that people of all religious persuasions, the vast majority of whom will have a highly favorable impression of Jesus, will marvel, as I have, at His masterful ministry to every human being He encountered.

A major aim of this book is to bring the accounts of Jesus' interactions from the pages of the New Testament and into our world. The section "Walk with Jesus" highlights the aspects of each spiritual profile that Jesus would commend, and others that would concern Him. Then I have a series of questions that Jesus might have asked if we lived in His day, and that I wish each reader will ask him- or herself today.

Jesus' short life on this earth catalyzed an ever-growing army of disciples who represent Him in our contemporary world. I hope those who read this book are, or will be, among them. So the section titled "Work for Jesus" addresses how we can represent Jesus wisely and well in the lives of people of differing spiritual profiles. In this way the work of Jesus continues and multiplies. This concluding portion of each chapter addresses seven issues:

1. *Making a connection.* Where and how did Jesus connect with this spiritual profile?

2. *The tone of the conversation.* Since so much communication happens nonverbally, what can we learn and apply from the tone of Jesus' interactions with this spiritual profile?

3. *Finding common ground.* Most effective connections with people happen when we find and stand on that which we hold in common rather than that which separates us. What common ground did Jesus find with each spiritual profile?

4. *Finding the lost and losing the found.* Some time ago, also while reading through the Gospels, a friend and I discovered that Jesus not only sought to "seek and save what was lost" (Luke 19:10), but also had to help the "found" get lost. Most of the people of Israel in Jesus' day (as in ours) regarded themselves as "children of God." When we examined every incident in the Gospels in which Jesus sought to bring people the good news, we discovered that in about 25 percent of the incidents He was trying to get lost people found, and in the rest Jesus was working to get found people lost. So how does Jesus do it?

5. *Surprisingly.* With each of the spiritual profiles Jesus says or does things that I found surprising . . . but very wise.

6. *Slogans and symbols.* Sometimes truth is best taught and caught in memorable "sound bites" or pictures. As one should expect of those who seek to represent the Master Teacher in the lives of others, slogans and symbols may well carry the day.

7. *Connecting with Jesus.* The ultimate aim of Jesus, and of this book, is to connect people with Jesus. Again, not surprisingly, Jesus, the "Man for all profiles," reveals Himself to people in each spiritual profile in ways that they will understand and will be particularly meaningful to them.

So, take the test and see who you resemble in Jesus' day. Get to know this group (and the other groups) better. Find out where they came from, what brought about their rise and fall, how they viewed life, and what was their worldview and lifestyle. Then ponder the incidents in the Gospels in which Jesus dealt with various spiritual profiles. Watch Him at work, marvel, and learn. Certainly you would have wanted to walk with Jesus if you had lived in His day. So consider how He might have approached you and what He would have wanted to talk about. Finally, take the challenge Jesus has given to each of His followers throughout time, and represent Him in the lives of others. Learn from His wise ways and follow in His footsteps.

Profile:
The Gentiles

The search for happiness is one of the chief sources of unhappiness.

—Eric Hoffer

JESUS *and the* UNCHURCHED

"Dad, I hate being a pastor's kid!" Obviously these were not the words I wanted to hear from my teenage son. I was stunned and troubled. So I asked him why.

"It's not you or the church, Dad. It's just that your job is so weird. People in school—when they find out my father is a minister—ask me if my dad knocks people over."

When he explained further, I realized that the only concept many of his classmates in public school had of Christian pastors was what they derived from televangelists. And by all accounts, these telecasts do not resemble normal church life. However, this is the only normalcy that many who never go to church know, or may ever know.

We don't need pollsters to tell us that the Christian church in the Western world is declining (while it happens to be growing in the southern hemisphere and Asia).[1] A poll by the Barna Group estimates the number of unchurched in the United States to be approaching 100 million, or about one-third of the American population.[2] This growing group includes two spiritual profiles I identify in chapters 1 and 2 of this book, the unchurched (or the Gentiles) and the detached (or the detached and disenfranchised Jews). The unchurched seldom, if ever, attend a Christian church. They may subscribe to another religion or no religion at all. They know very little experientially about the beliefs, rituals, rules, or behaviors of churched people. For the most part the church is irrelevant to them.

In Jesus' day there were no churches, so the unchurched were really the "unsynagogued," that is, the "Gentiles"[3] (*goyim*). From a Jewish perspective, the Gentiles came into existence the day God called Abram to be the first Jew (Genesis 12), around 2,000 BC. Ever since that time, Jews and Gentiles have always lived around each other, but usually remained distinct from one another.

INTRODUCING THE GENTILES

When God called out the first Jew, Abram (Genesis 11), and made a covenant with him (Genesis 12), He stated that "all peoples on earth will be blessed through you" (v. 3). Thus began an unbalanced division of humanity into two groups, a minuscule people group called the "Jews" and a mammoth group called "Gentiles."

It is almost comical to devote only one spiritual profile to the Gentiles when technically they make up more than 99 percent of the population of the world. In Bible times the Gentiles were everybody who wasn't a Jew, and yet, the Bible overwhelmingly highlights the history of the Jews. Nevertheless, Gentiles figured prominently in the Old Testament and the New.

Throughout the Old Testament, Gentiles are mentioned. We first meet the Canaanites, who interacted with the patriarchs; then the Egyptians, who enslaved the Hebrews; and the Midianites, with whom Moses lived. We encounter the uncircumcised Philistines, who for so many years were Israel's nemesis; the Phoenicians, who gave supplies for the building of the temple; and the Syrian general Naaman, who was healed of leprosy. Then we meet a succession of Gentile nations who subdue the Jews, including the Egyptians, Assyrians, Babylonians, Medes and Persians, Greeks, and Romans. Though the Jews were selected as God's "chosen people," the Gentiles have always been on His divine radar.[4]

Many Gentiles in Jesus' day lived in Israel. Most were part of the far-flung Roman Empire that stretched from the

Atlantic Ocean to the Euphrates River. Since Israel was a natural land bridge between the three continents comprising the Empire, Gentiles crisscrossed the country constantly, and many chose to settle down, seizing opportunities for agriculture (especially in Galilee) and commerce. Israel was indeed a major crossroads of the world.

Economically the Gentiles in Israel came from all classes from nobility to slaves, from ladder-climbing military personnel to those caught in the nonpersonhood of slavery. And of course, most had no interest in the Jewish synagogue, although proselytes could enter the court of the Gentiles. Almost all were polytheistic, and many worshiped the Roman gods of the day. Let's look more closely at the Gentiles' TENDENCIES.

TENDENCIES of the "Unsynagogued" Gentiles

Truth: The source of truth to the first-century Gentile was a hodgepodge of polytheistic myths and legends, pagan superstitions, Hellenistic philosophy, and Latin law. Some would also have had familiarity with the Hebrew Scriptures.

Economics: Gentile society in Jesus' day was divided into a variety of classes based on birth, wealth, and ethnic background. Many Gentiles were slaves and a large disparity separated rich and poor. The Romans had developed a sophisticated market economy based on agriculture, trade, mining, manufacturing, and government projects. Rome imposed a heavy tax on the Judea province to fund the governmental portion of the economy.

N*eighborhood:* The Gentiles' sense of community was strong. Its basis was the extended family, which was loyal to the city-state, which was a part of the greater Roman Empire. State religion was the glue that held it all together.

D*evotion:* Tapping the power of the gods to live a good and happy life was a Gentile pursuit. The gods were feared and fate was assumed. Thus keeping on the good side of the gods was all important. This was accomplished by participation in various religious ceremonies and making appropriate sacrifices.

E*veryman:* The Gentiles, borrowing from the Greeks, separated the soul from the body, matter from spirit. They believed that every person had a divine soul, and an imprisoning body. Cultivation of the soul was emphasized, even as what one did with his body was deemphasized. Choosing to accept one's fate and make the most of it was the route to happiness.

N*ature of God:* The Gentiles feared and worshiped a pantheon of gods that they believed gave them peace and prosperity. Patriotism, religion, and superstition were combined, and the power of the gods was more important than the gods' character.

Civics: The synthesis of religion and state was assumed by the normal Gentile. The gods were intertwined with politics, and the emperor was somewhat deified. Submission to the Roman government and law was considered a sacred civic duty. And for most Gentiles the benefits of Roman rule were considerable (heavy taxation excluded, of course).

Immortality: The Gentiles widely believed in an afterlife. However, its existence was shadowy and the fear of the unknown was very strong. Most expected a time of judgment, followed by a spirit existence in the underworld. The specially virtuous or heroic could expect their souls to rest in better place, like the Elysian Fields.

Ethics: The Roman world was built on law more than morality.[5] Right and wrong was determined by the law of the state, not by philosophical notions of virtue or religious notions of morality. If the laws of the state, designed largely to keep the peace and enhance prosperity, did not preclude an activity, it was not considered wrong. Thus, moral corruption, particularly in the sexual realm, was common and not considered unethical.

Summary: The Gentiles in Jesus' day were largely god-fearing people. Belief in the gods dominated their thinking, and keeping on the good side of the gods dominated their behavior (superstitions, omens, traditions, rituals, rites, taboos, etc.). They also wanted to enjoy life. Thus sports, entertainment, and the pursuit of pleasure were their goals. And all of these were with a view to living a good, happy life on earth and the hope of a peaceful rest in the next world.

WATCH JESUS

How did Jesus interact with the Gentiles in His day? Consider these seven encounters.

Foreign Forbearers
(Jesus and His Gentile Roots)

Jesus' first "interaction" with the Gentiles occurs centuries before He is born. The New Testament opens with His genealogy (Matthew 1:1–17). Jesus' family tree connects Him with the first Jew, Abraham; the Jewish patriarchs; the greatest Jewish king, David; and numerous other famous—and infamous—and unknown Jews. Jesus' roots are undeniably Jewish. However, one cannot fail to notice that Jesus' genealogy also includes Gentiles. Three Gentile women, two of them known for their sexual immorality (Tamar in Genesis 38 and Rahab) and one for her love (Ruth), are listed among Jesus' forebearers. The very first thing the gospels highlight about the Gentiles is that Jesus had "bad"

Gentile blood! Conspicuously Jesus identified with all humanity, "the good, the bad and the ugly."

"Galilee of the Gentiles"
(Gentile Neighbors)

After a brief sojourn in Africa (Matthew 2:13), the holy family moves back to Nazareth, to "Galilee of the Gentiles" (Matthew 4:15, quoting Isaiah 9:1). Jesus spends roughly the next thirty years of His life in Nazareth, a small town, likely inhabited mostly by Jews. However, He may have worked, and surely He shopped, in Sepphoris, a sophisticated Roman city about four miles northwest of Nazareth. Galilee is racially mixed, mainly Greek-speaking, has a large number of slaves, and is less than one-third Jewish. Important trade routes crisscross Galilee. As a result, Gentile merchants, soldiers, and travelers frequent the region. Jesus would rub shoulders with Europeans (Romans, Greeks, etc.), Middle Eastern Asians (Phoenicians, Syrians, Persians, etc.), and Africans (Egyptians, Libyans, etc.).

Though never explicitly stated, Jesus must have maintained cordial relationships with His Gentile workmates, customers, neighbors, and passersby. I fully suspect, that as a good Jew, Jesus did quality work, treated His customers fairly, was a good neighbor, and extended a typical Middle-Eastern hand of hospitality to strangers. We can reasonably surmise that Jesus developed and maintained mutually respectful relationships with the Gentiles in His life.

Going to the Dogs
(The Canaanite Woman)

Calling someone a "dog" is derogatory worldwide today, but it was doubly so in Jesus' day. Back then dogs were unclean scavengers (cf. Exodus 22:31; 1 Samuel 24:14), and to call someone a "dog" was a term of deep contempt. So, Jesus' encounter with the Canaanite woman in Phoenicia (Matthew 15:21–28; Mark 7:24–30) adds spice and significance to His ministry among the Gentiles while it plays with the word "dog."

The story begins with the bland-sounding words, "He entered a house" (Mark 7:24). However, in His day it might have been said, "Jesus has gone to the dogs!" Gentiles are "dogs" by common Jewish estimation. In the house, Jesus is approached by a Syrophoenician woman who has a demonized daughter. Thus, she has three strikes against her: her race (a Gentile), her heritage (a history of conflicts with the Jews), and her problem (a demonized daughter).

Jesus' exchange with the woman is classic. He baits her by suggesting that "it is not right to take the children's bread" (God's covenantal priority on the Jews) and "toss it to their dogs" (Gentiles).[6] She unhesitatingly acknowledged her second-class status, then added that she would settle for some covenantal "crumbs." She will gladly "dumpster dive" to provide "food" for her daughter. Jesus is thoroughly impressed with her humility and faith. When we watch Jesus at work, we notice that He sometimes waited for human resources to be exhausted, bootstraps to break, hopes to be dashed, and "crumbs" to become desirable before He stepped forward with good news and good deeds.

Food Fight
(Gentiles and Food)

The juxtaposition of Jesus confronting the issue of food laws (Mark 7:1–23) and His visit with the Syrophoenician woman (Mark 7:24–30) is by no means accidental. Jewish food laws created significant barriers, and Jesus knows that leaving such barriers in place will waylay His mission to the world. So Jesus emphatically states, "Nothing outside a man can make him 'unclean'" (Mark 7:15). And Mark makes the implications of Jesus' words plain as day, "In saying this, Jesus declared all foods 'clean'" (Mark 7:19).

The fight over food essentially separates Jews and Gentiles, and the early Christian church cannot shake it until God shakes up Peter and causes him to reconsider his perspective on food (Acts 10). And even with God's clear instructions to guide them, the church still struggles mightily with food issues throughout the remainder of New Testament times (Acts 15; Romans 14–15; 1 Corinthians 8; Revelation 2:14, 20). When we watch Jesus at work among the Gentiles, we notice that He busted barriers that would have impeded the spread of the gospel.

Interview Request Denied
(The Greeks)

During the week of Jesus' crucifixion, some Greeks (Gentile God-fearers) who have come to Jerusalem to celebrate the Passover, request an interview with Jesus (John 12:20–36). Jesus, however, is focused on the cross, and appears to ignore their request. Instead Jesus launches into a monologue on the cost and glory of His impending death.

It strikes me as strange that this incident is even mentioned. So why is it? When we watch Jesus at work, we notice that He is very sensitive to divine timing. Sometimes we try to push God's work when the time is not right and the people are not ripe. Sometimes we are too afraid to let Gentile appetites intensify and thirsts get to a parched pitch without providing gospel crumbs and sips. Sometimes we seem to act as if our job is to kick-start the dead, or manipulate the mellow, or persuade the indifferent, or drop the whole load on the merely curious. We are afraid to let people get thoroughly lost. Jesus refused to "sell the divine" before its time.

Sadistic Soldiers

(The Roman Executioners)

Not all Gentiles are as guileless as the good Gentiles we have met thus far in the gospels. Some are downright diabolical.[7] In Matthew 27:27–31 we find a group of Gentile soldiers making sport of Jesus. Seven *S* words tell a story of incredible sadism: "they stripped him," they "put a scarlet robe on him," they "set it [a crown of thorns] on his head," they "put a staff in his right hand," they said "Hail, king of the Jews!", "they spit on him," and they "took the staff and struck him on the head again and again."

The divide between the genuine seekers and the skillful sadists seems to be accentuated by the person of Jesus. When we watch Jesus at work with the Gentiles, we notice that some see nothing special about Him. He is just a common criminal executed in a day's work. Many "Gentiles" are so fixated on the pursuit of their own stuff that they see nothing special in Jesus—much to their eternal loss.

Divine Death

(Two Roman Centurions)

The Bible is surprisingly full of military personnel who are godly.[8] The first one Jesus meets is a Roman centurion whose servant is paralyzed at home (Matthew 8:5–13; Luke 7:1–10). The final centurion He meets is watching His execution (Mark 15:39).

The first centurion addresses Jesus as "Lord" and regards Jesus' time as highly valuable. The centurion defies our typical image of a pagan soldier. He is spiritually attuned, neither macho nor self-centered, and he is humble and trusting. Gentile respect for genuine religion is often greater than is supposed. While the centurion is mindful of the religious barriers that traditionally separate Jews and Gentiles, Jesus seems oblivious to them. In fact, before the centurion encounter, Jesus aids a leper (Matthew 8:1–4) and afterward, a woman.[9] When we watch Jesus at work with the Gentiles we notice that He notices some of the ingredients of genuine seeking faith: brokenness, humility, and trust.

The second centurion probably has seen many men die. Certainly he has heard some vile language and seen his share of vicious people. I suppose he has witnessed a few good people die as well. But the centurion has never seen anyone die like Jesus!

What is it about the death of Jesus that so moves this military man? Is it Jesus' words? Certainly the seven statements Jesus made while on the cross are unique. Is it the juxtaposition of events (Passover, earthquake, darkness, veil rip, etc.)? Certainly these events would have given even a cynical soldier pause. Was it Jesus' demeanor? Probably few of the executed had been taunted by such an eclectic and powerful crowd. Whatever the reasons, he came to a surprising conclusion, "Surely he was the Son of God!"

(Matthew 27:54; cf. Mark 15:39), and "Surely this was a righteous man" (Luke 23:47). When we watch Jesus at work with the Gentiles, we notice that how Jesus died spoke volumes to those who would listen.

WALK WITH JESUS

What might Jesus want to discuss with us if we had the opportunity to take a walk with Him? How might Jesus interact with Gentile-like people today—those who are unchurched and seemingly disinterested in the one true God?

In keeping with His style in the book of Revelation (Revelation 2–3), Jesus would likely highlight some commendable traits and then identify some danger spots. Additionally, He would likely ask some penetrating questions.

I suspect that Jesus would cherish the opportunity of talking "religion" with someone who didn't have a lot to unlearn, and didn't think they had all the answers. Surely, Jesus would not be shocked that Gentiles behave like Gentiles. I suspect He would not cringe when they cursed, nor glare when they told a dirty joke, nor scowl when they made mistakes, nor say "I told you so" when they poured out the pain their own sin had caused. And this would come as a huge relief to those who may fear the God-with-the-baseball-bat.

Jesus would also, no doubt, have a few Gentile critiques. He could go on all day, if He wished, about the countless times and occasions when they have ignored His Spirit that tried to convict them of "sin and righteousness and judgment" (John 16:8) in order to lead them to the cross. Every day in every way God had been working to draw them but with innumerable excuses and self-justifications they refused to be broken. He might point out how time after time they have unwittingly given the Devil an open door to their souls. He might also point out how the consequences of their sin were designed to produce brokenness not bitterness and blaming. Why were they not more cynical about following the spirit of their age?

What questions would Jesus want to talk about with Gentile-like, unchurched people today? Here are several He might ask the unchurched:

- Have you ever investigated your spiritual roots? What do you think you'd find?
- What do you see when you look at the stars?
- When favorable coincidences or serendipities occur, who do you thank?
- Have you ever made fun of or mistreated a Christian who tried to tell you about Me?
- Where do you go, or to what do you turn, to soothe or silence your soul pain?
- Who do you look up to as a hero?

* Where are you looking for happiness? How successful to date is your pursuit of happiness?
* Where do you turn, to whom do you run, when you face a tragedy?
* With whom do you feel safe?
* Have you ever wished you had an open, honest relationship with a pastor or other religious person?
* What has been the return on your investment in politics?

WORK FOR JESUS

How can we be more useful in representing Jesus to people we meet who in background and outlook are Gentile-like? Here are seven areas to consider as you interact with the unchurched.

1. Making a Connection

Jesus connected with the Gentiles by simply sharing geography and life with them. Jesus' best friends were Jewish, but He grew up among Gentiles. Jesus stated that His priority was to bring the good news of the kingdom to His people, the Jews. Nevertheless, when Gentiles came to Him, Jesus connected naturally and lovingly with them. I suspect that Jesus had a good reputation among the Gentiles in Galilee. Though Jesus didn't focus on the Gentiles,

He always seemed to be comfortable with them and was completely authentic around them.

If we are going to represent Jesus among those who have no familiarity with church or religion, we are going to have to build natural, mutually respectful, and trustworthy relationships. A deeply damaging mentality to the cause of Christ is to treat unchurched people as projects rather than people. If we have ulterior motives for friendship, Gentiles will often "smell a rat"—and should!

As Jesus' representatives, we must build bridges of availability. We must choose to err on the side of generosity. Somehow we must learn to be like Jesus. We should neither wince nor wink at sin. Jesus was particularly tuned in to the spiritual needs of the Gentiles. He saw their emptiness, their thirst, the fear, the hope. We should sow seeds all the time. God will work to make them germinate. It takes water and heat for a seed to break its shell and start to germinate. Build relationships, build bridges, build common ground so that when the "mud hits the fan" they will think of and come to you.

2. The Tone of the Conversation

Elusive is the word that comes to mind when I think of Jesus' interactions with the Gentiles. However, Jesus is not elusive in the sense of trying to avoid the Gentiles. Rather Jesus seems elusive in that He makes them curious, makes them come to Him, and makes them initiate the interaction. All my life I have heard the line to "go" and take the gospel to those who have never heard. While this is obviously a good thing to do, it may slightly miss the genius of Jesus. Not infrequently, I have tried to share the good news about Jesus with people who didn't care or weren't ready. I then characteristically chalked it up to either their spiritual indifference or my evangelistic ineptitude. Maybe it was neither. Maybe, motivated by the laudable desire for people to come to the Savior, I had failed to lean on the Holy Spirit, whose job it is to make people thirsty. Jesus almost seems to "play hard to get" with the Gentiles.

Sometimes we are so intent on getting people saved that we forget that only God can do that. Perhaps we would be better representatives of Jesus if we followed His methods and His lead with the unchurched.

3. Finding Common Ground

Most of Jesus' interactions with the Gentiles had some physical dimension to them. The gospel story begins with a list of Jesus' physical descendants. Then we learn that the Word of God took on a physical body to live among us (John 1:1, 14). And where did He live? He lived primarily within physical proximity of the Gentiles. The Gentiles came to Jesus primarily with physical needs (including paralysis, cutting, and demonization), and Jesus refused to let food separate Him from the Gentiles. It is Jesus' physical crucifixion that brings Pilate, Herod, and the soldiers into the story. Jesus' physical death moves the centurion to faith, and it is the physical evidence of Jesus' resurrection that turns the world upside down.

Physical preoccupation seems to be quintessentially "Gentile." If so, we must live in an increasingly Gentile culture. Preoccupation with the body seems to be a priority. Our media is dominated by physical images. We worship body types and talents. Vast markets are geared toward body comforts and relieving bodily pain. And we have come to believe that satisfying and satiating bodily needs is the route to happiness. I suppose we can lament the superficiality of this preoccupation. Or we can work with it—as Jesus did.

The Gentiles were, and are, "show me" people. They had tangible needs and required solid evidence. As has been often said, faith is only as good as its object. That may be a key reason the historically best-attested gospel event is Jesus' Passion—His crucifixion, burial, and resurrection. For all Gentiles there is as solid historical evidence for the physical facts of Jesus' life, death, and resurrection as there is for any other historical event in antiquity.

Those who represent Jesus must be in the business of meeting physical needs. We pray for God's power to heal the physically sick, and in the meantime we seek to relieve their pain and provide comfort. We use some of our resources to meet the physical needs of the poor and suffering. We increase thirst by living salty lives (Matthew 5:13), and light by doing good deeds (vv. 14–16). We must let our lights so shine that those in our circle of association will feel free to come to us for help and answers when their lights are punched out by life.

4. Finding the Lost

How did Jesus seek and find the lost Gentiles? Generally He didn't! Part of this omission may be due to His unique status and mission. However, part of it may have been a ministry strategy. Jesus, by my reckoning, never went to a Gentile —they always came to Him. But He was constantly rubbing shoulders with Gentiles: they knew who He was, where they could find Him, and how He would receive them.

John was my neighbor, and one of the last people I would have imagined showing up at church. He was in his eighties, having been married multiple times, and now living with a woman to whom he was not married. Still, we chatted numerous times on the street in front of our houses. The talk was always superficial, but the trust was slowly building. Then one afternoon while walking past his house the week after Easter, John stopped me and said, "Tom, I really liked your talk on Easter." As I said, John was not a likely churchgoer.

Since John opened the door to the conversation, I decided to take the next step. So I asked him, "Would you like to talk more about it?"

John's answer was abrupt, "No, I don't want to talk because I'm a very bad person." Before I had a chance to reply, he remarked, "But you can count on seeing me in church again next year."

Sure enough, next year John was there. And so I expected to see him again come the third year. A relative informed me, however, that John was in the hospital, so I went to see him on Easter Sunday afternoon. This time he wanted to talk. He started to tell me about some of the bad things he had done, and the list was long. He had a deep sense that God couldn't forgive him. I told him otherwise. And John took God's Word for it. Within days John died, as peaceful a death as I have ever witnessed.

5. Surprisingly . . .

A few things surprised me when I looked at all of Jesus' interactions with the Gentiles. One, I was surprised by how few interactions there were. Galilee, where Jesus spent most of His time ministering, was mostly Gentile. Moreover, Capernaum, Jesus' ministry headquarters, was along a road frequented by Gentiles. Thus, most of the people Jesus laid eyes on were probably Gentiles, and yet the Gospels record very little interaction with them. Almost every Gentile in the Gospels who came to Jesus was richly rewarded for his or her efforts. So why didn't more come? And why didn't Jesus go to them?

If I was Jesus, and thankfully I am not, I would more actively have pursued the Gentiles to try to teach His disciples the importance of getting the gospel out to the world. After all, it took almost ten years after Jesus left this world for the disciples to get the message that God wanted the message to go to the whole world. And still it took a thrice-repeated vision to Peter and a knock to the ground for Paul to get it.

Two, I was surprised by the depth of Gentile faith having such limited knowledge of God. Rahab and Ruth, part of Old Testament history, reappear in Jesus' genealogy, setting an incredible standard for largely ignorant Gentiles acknowledging the true God. The magi, watching only the heavens, set out on a long journey to find and worship the newborn king. The faith of the centurion and the Canaanite woman elicit high praise from Jesus. And the centurion at the cross utters a highly advanced evaluation of the identity of Jesus. The Gentiles don't seem to have as many preconceived notions about the Messiah, so they are relatively quick to acknowledge Him often with great faith and breathtaking insight.

Third, Jesus' lack of "cultural relevance" with the Gentiles is surprising. Much of the Western church today is on a cultural relevance kick. Give the culture what it wants with a little Jesus thrown in. Be positive, be humorous, be "lite," speak their language, frequent their haunts and attend their parties, keep up with their media, entertainment, and sports. And do all this in order to reach them with the gospel. But Jesus doesn't strike me as being very Gentile friendly. He basically ignores them, almost talks down to them, speaks seldom to them, is not very funny with them, doesn't offer "bread and circuses." He does, however, offer life!

6. Slogans and Symbols

The common athletic slogan "No Pain, No Gain" seems to fit the Gentiles perfectly. They undoubtedly prefer "It's All about You" or "Just Do It" or "Play More."[10] However, most of the Gentiles who interacted with Jesus either experienced great pain or observed it. And in many cases, it was this pain that became a severe mercy.

Those who are outside the church likewise feel or have observed great pain. Be sensitive to it. I keep a running list of men I know who, beyond the age of thirty, have become faithful followers of Jesus. Every one of them on the list, with a single exception, has come to Christ out of deep pain, most often a bitter divorce. I cannot speak for all of them, but some I know have found that the pain so broke them that they had nowhere to go but to Jesus. They gained Christ!

7. Connecting with Jesus

Jesus characteristically sought to connect each spiritual profile with Himself in terms and concepts they understood. The two titles most often on the mouths of the Gentiles with whom Jesus interacts are: "Son of" and "King of." Gentiles understood sons and kings. "Sons" carried the idea of special relationship and "kings" carried the idea of exalted position. Jesus wanted the Gentiles to come to know Him as the "Son of Man," one with whom they could relate on every level; the "King of the Jews," one who would usher in peace and justice; and the "Son of God," one who could represent them before God. In Jesus of Nazareth they got all three.

Hanging in my office is a print of a painting by Norman Rockwell entitled "Sunday Morning." The artist depicts a father slumped in his chair, still wearing his pajamas, smoking a cigarette, reading the sports page of the newspaper, hair resembling the horns of the devil, and eyes upraised in a look of guilt and disdain. In the background, the man's wife and three children, dressed in their Sunday best, file past his chair on their way to church. All three females have slightly elevated noses in a pious posture with their Bibles in hand. The lone male, however, the youngest in the picture, looks longingly at Dad. If only Dad knew there was another Son who longed to know him too.

Profile:
The Detached Jews

There lives more faith in honest doubt, Believe me, than in half the creeds.

—ALFRED LORD TENNYSON

2

JESUS *and the* DETACHED

George was raised in a good fundamentalist Christian home, and he was a close family friend. He went to church, found a job, got married, had some children, and drifted away from church. Maybe it was his smoking and drinking that raised eyebrows and made him feel uncomfortable around church people. Maybe it was his cussing and carousing that made him feel like a hypocrite going to church. Well, he knew most of them were hypocrites too. Maybe it was the lure of easy money that captured his time and attention.

Whatever the reason, George found church increasingly

unpleasant and irrelevant. So he dropped out. And frankly, he didn't miss it a bit.

George pursued the "good life." Money became his new god. The economy was good at the time, and with some help from his friends, including my father, George put together a thriving business. He was real good at making deals. In fact, George was so good at making money that he built his dream house, with an indoor swimming pool. As the money flowed, God and church became distant memories. He no longer needed them.

George is by no means alone. A fast-growing segment of the American population would now be classified as "dechurched." These people, unlike the unchurched we met in the previous chapter, have some familiarity with church. They understand the rules, rhythms, and rituals of church life. And they may occasionally "pop in" for special occasions and when they feel like it. But most of the time they don't. They are the detached and the dechurched.

How do the unchurched differ from the dechurched? How do the Gentiles differ from the "lost sheep of the House of Israel"? Let me suggest five telling differences: First, the Gentiles/unchurched are generally clueless about religious concepts and lingo; whereas the "lost sheep" understand the words and basic concepts. Second, the Gentiles may not like the religious, and are highly suspicious of the religious, but they have probably not been directly hurt by the religious; whereas the lost sheep generally carry some baggage of hurt. Third, the Gentiles certainly have consciences and have a sense of right and wrong, yet they generally are not plagued by guilt; whereas the lost sheep of Israel are burdened by it. Fourth, the Gentiles may go to a religious building for some gathering without emotional attachment; whereas the lost sheep generally will experience considerable emotion (usually negative) when they go. Finally, the Gentiles view the religious with distant curiosity and perhaps disdain; whereas the lost sheep relate to the religious body as a rejected lover would.

The reasons people drop out of church are legion. Some have been hurt or lost hope, or found their expectations unmet, or found their participation unwanted or unappreciated. Many have gotten caught up in a church fight—a nasty business indeed. A pastor perhaps got on a power trip, or he tripped up, or someone thought he did. Perhaps it was a building program, financial irregularities, or personality clashes. Others simply decided church didn't meet their needs, solve their problems, or add any value to their lives. And then there are those faithful souls who gave their heart and soul to the church but got used, abused, and burned out. They're not so faithful anymore. As I said, the reasons are too many to list.[1] Whatever the reasons, people find that the church does not provide the sense of meaning, connectedness, and usefulness they seek. These are the detached.

INTRODUCING THE DETACHED JEWS

From the time of Abraham to today, the Jewish people have always included a significant segment that could be called "secular Jews,"² or as Jesus called them, "lost sheep" (Matthew 10:5–6; 15:24). Though the Jews are widely credited with giving the world the great gift of monotheism, some have always drifted toward a secular lifestyle that ignored God's law and behaved as if God did not exist.³

Let me cite three Old Testament examples. Esau was born into the first family of faith but became oblivious to God. He was a man's man, but doesn't seem to be a God-oriented man (Genesis 25:19–28). Esau was a man of his appetites, who sold his birthright for a bowl of lentils (Genesis 25:29–34), which the writer of Hebrews describes as "godless" (Hebrews 12:16–17). Meanwhile, Samson was born to godly parents but became a product of his godless age (Judges 13–16; 17:6; 21:25). His life was dominated by uncontrolled sexual addiction. Even though God's Spirit empowered Samson's exploits, he seemed oblivious (until the end of his life) to God's presence, power, or demands on his life.

Third, consider the Jews depicted in the book of Esther. The Jewish people never do anything at the core of the

law (even when it would have been most natural and pro-
pitious to do so) and do several things expressly forbidden.
The heroes of the story, Esther and Mordecai, are secular
Jews who have found a new home among the Persian
people. Although Esther is indeed a model of courage, she
most certainly is not a model of godliness.[4] Esther is a secular Jew. The point of the book, centering around the Feast
of Purim ("Dice"), is that God is faithful to His people
even when His people forget Him.

After the time of Esther and before the arrival of Jesus
(known as the Intertestamental Period), three powerful
movements impacted the people of Israel in a manner that
challenged their fidelity to God and His law: Hellenism,
the Hasmoneans, and Herod.

Hellenism, the "devotion to or imitation of ancient
Greek thought, customs, or styles,"[5] was part of the legacy
of Alexander the Great's conquest of Israel (in 333–332
BC). Greek influence was still potent in Jesus' day. A sizeable portion of Jews in Israel found the Hellenistic worldview and lifestyle to be very attractive.

However, the push by the Syrian overlords of Israel in
the second-century BC to Hellenize the country gave rise
to a backlash of Jewish patriotism called the Maccabean
Revolt (167–164 BC). Using guerrilla tactics, the Jewish
patriots, led by Mattathias Maccabeus, overthrew the Hellenists and established the Hasmonean Dynasty that was

to rule Israel for the next one hundred years (164–63 BC). Ironically, the Hasmoneans, who began as an anti-Hellenistic movement, eventually came to embrace many of the tenets of Hellenism. So now some of the Jewish leadership of Israel was thoroughly Hellenized.

Hasmonean rule lasted until 63 BC when Judea was conquered by the Roman army. Then in 37 BC King Herod the Great entered the scene. Though claiming Jewish kinship, Herod was first a Roman. During his tenure as "King of the Jews" he administered effectively, built magnificently, and ruled ruthlessly. Herod and his family dominated the political landscape of Israel during Jesus' life and the apostolic age and promoted Roman culture. The Jews who followed and/or worked for Herod's government were called Herodians. They are not mentioned outside the Gospels. Being Jewish and loyal to Herod brought both benefits and risks. The benefits were largely economic and the risks were primarily social and religious. Loyalty to Herod brought jobs and money. And loyalty to Herod brought hatred and ostracism. A typical Herodian job in Jesus' day would be collecting taxes or working in the governmental bureaucracy. This job in any country is somewhat despised, but is hated when the taxes go to an occupying and pagan government.

So, when Jesus began His public ministry in Israel around AD 30, many Jewish people were effectively detached from the mainstream religious life of the nation. These lost sheep included those who followed in the footsteps of Esau, Samson, and Esther; Jews indeed, but not religiously observant Jews. And the lost sheep included Hellenists, whose embrace of Greek culture made them outsiders; Herodians, whose association with the Roman government made them suspect and outcasts; and those I call hellions, or "sinners," whose lifestyle choices made them pariahs.

How does one become a lost sheep today? It is a process. Probably a lost sheep was raised in the religious body or at some point became connected with it. Maybe they were raised in a religious home, or educated at a religious school, or became involved in a religious children's ministry or youth group. Perhaps as an adult he or she enjoyed for a time the life of the religious organization. Then something happened. Perhaps he felt unwanted or unneeded, even invisible. Perhaps she got burned or burned out, or any of the other traumas noted on page 49. Gradually they drifted away or abruptly they left. They came to the conclusion that "I don't need this." "I can be spiritual without being religious." "I don't have to be a part of organized religion to have a relationship with God." And in some cases, they did something stupid, something immoral or unlawful, and became persona non grata in the religious assembly.

TENDENCIES of the Detached Jews

Truth: Though raised with a religious moral code derived from Scripture and tradition, the Jewish "lost sheep" find their truth in other sources as well, including economics, philosophy, and perceived self-interest.

Economics: Ostracized by the religious mainstream, and motivated by the lure of money, the "lost sheep" Jews pursued material gain, and some were highly successful at it. Working for the Romans had its financial perks.

Neighborhood: The "lost sheep" Jews seemed to have no lack of friends, generally people like themselves. Those who were not welcome in the religious establishment tended to band together in their place of business and their homes.

Devotion: The "lost sheep" Jews had detached themselves, or been detached from, the normal practice of religion in Israel. They may well have retained a personalized spiritual life (including showing up at temple and praying), but they had effectively dropped out of organized religion.

Everyman: The detached Jews probably reacted against the notion that nonreligious people are bad. They see themselves and their friends as basically good people, in spite of their flaws. Readily they would admit that "nobody's perfect."

N*ature of God:* Those who have walked away from organized religion usually retain a sense of God, and oftentimes the guilt that accompanies a certain concept of God, but choose to relate to Him in their own way outside the rituals and rules. They hope God is forgiving.

C*ivics:* In the battle between church and state, this group would support the state. Not only did the Romans keep the peace and keep bread on the table, but they also didn't seem any more corrupt than the Jewish leaders.

I*mmortality:* Their attitude was, Who knows what happens when a person dies? Hope for the best.

E*thics:* The detached tended to find and follow their own moral compass. And that compass generally pointed to what they perceived to be in their personal best interest.

S*ummary:* "Follow the money" might be an appropriate slogan of the lost sheep.

WATCH JESUS

How did Jesus interact with the secular Jews in His day? Consider these eight encounters.

Dinner with the Sinners
(Matthew)

Few occupations in Jesus' day were more despised than that of the tax man. So, interestingly, Jesus' first recorded interaction with "lost sheep" takes place at a tax booth[6] and subsequently at Matthew's house (Matthew 9:9–13; Mark 2:14–17; Luke 5:27–32). Matthew is a pariah to his fellow Jews, as are Matthew's "sinner" friends. But not to Jesus. Jesus initiates the interaction, accepts a dinner invitation (a stunning statement of acceptance), and seems to thoroughly enjoy the conversation. When questioned about His questionable choice of friends, Jesus shoots back with biting sarcasm. When we watch Jesus at work with detached Jews, we notice several startling strategies. One, He goes to them on their turf, where they feel comfortable. Two, Jesus seems to enjoy their company, and they enjoy His. Three, Jesus doesn't bring up the subject of sin, but when His critics do, He redefines and deepens it. Sin is not so much breaking a law as it is refusing to see how much you are broken. And four, He redefines the place, the priority, and the purpose of ministry.

You Are Who You . . .
(The Sinners)

Type "You are who you . . ." into an Internet search engine and see what comes up. "You are who you eat with . . . work with . . . associate with . . . hang out with." If these adages are altogether true, Jesus was in a heap of trouble. "Sinners" in Jesus' day were those who did not keep the law of Moses. And because Jesus hung out with such people,

He naturally acquired the "sinner" label (Matthew 11:19).

Religious people are particularly prone to "You are who you . . ." thinking. And, of course, there are Bible verses (strikingly taken out of context) to support this. "Bad company corrupts good character" (1 Corinthians 15:33; cf. Proverbs 22:24–25) and "Abstain from all appearance of evil" (1 Thessalonians 5:22 KJV) are regularly cited as proof texts. Had Jesus followed these adages, He would never have spent so much time with such disreputable people.

Perhaps Jesus would offer another adage for us to chew on and apply: "You are not who you think you are." It is instructive that the world's only sinless one freely associated with "sinners," was apparently openly accepted by "sinners," and was utterly untainted by their sin; in fact, they frequently came to acknowledge their sin and turn from it.

Poolside Problems
(The Disabled Man)

The disabled man at the Pool of Bethesda doesn't seem too clued in or connected when he has an encounter with Jesus (John 5:1–15). Through no fault of his own, the man at the pool appears to be a nonobservant Jew. He probably believes the local superstition that the waters of the pool had curative powers, but he didn't have friends to help him get in. And after he is healed by Jesus—on the Sabbath—he doesn't seem too aware of the Sabbath restrictions. He is,

I think, a lost sheep. Moreover, the disabled man never seeks out Jesus' help in the first place (he may not have even wanted to get well), he doesn't express any faith in Jesus, nor does he appear to want to know more about Jesus after his healing (Jesus found him).

Jesus warns the man about his sin, but apparently gets no response. When we watch Jesus at work among the detached Jews, we notice that He is neither soft on sin, nor surprised by indifference.

Crashing the Party
(The Sinful Woman)

A pattern of Jesus' interactions with the lost sheep seems to be developing. Namely, most of Jesus' interactions take place in homes. While a guest at the home of Simon the Pharisee, Jesus interacts with a "woman who had lived a sinful life"—on her initiation, not Simon's or Jesus' (Luke 7:36–37). The woman in the account never says a word and is only identified as a sinner. Certainly this means that her lifestyle is considered unacceptable to the religious. Certainly she has been excluded from the synagogue. And certainly she sees herself as a social and spiritual outcast. However, what she has greatly impresses Jesus. She has the courage to barge into a meal at a religious person's house. She has the confidence that Jesus will receive her kindly. She has the humility to throw inhibitions to the wind in order to visibly honor one she believed could forgive her. She has the honesty to see herself as broken. And she knows that no amount of money is large enough to pay for one who can heal her soul.[7]

And how does Jesus respond to this well-known sinner? He knows her past but sees past it. He sees her love and loves it. He sees her brokenness and forgives it. He sees her faith and rewards it. The contrast between Jesus and Simon the Pharisee could not be starker (7:38–50). Simon fixates on her sinful past; Jesus sees her future potential. Simon senses that his sins are minor, and thereby, according to Jesus, this stifles his affection for Jesus. Simon sees himself as relatively whole, and thus is unknowingly outside the reach of God's mercy. The woman sees herself as horribly broken, and thus a candidate for God's forgiveness. How ironic!

The Hellion
(Mary Magdalene)

The name of this detached Jew is the stuff of legend, fiction, and ridiculous speculation. Ask almost any Christian to tell you what they know about Mary Magdalene, and they will likely say she was a prostitute. Actually, there is no evidence of such. What she was, however, was worse. She had sold her soul to the Devil (Luke 8:2).

For all the press she has received through the years, there is precious little in the Scriptures about Mary. Prior to the resurrection, all we know about Mary is her very common name; her hometown, Magdala; her financial status (able to support Jesus and the disciples out of her private resources); and her spiritual condition—at one point fully demonized (Luke 8:1–3). That's it!

Everyone who is familiar with the passion of Jesus knows that Mary Magdalene is specially selected by Jesus to be the first witness of the resurrection.[8] Quite an honor indeed! Isn't it ironic that one who once had been fully demonized becomes a fully devoted follower of Jesus. And one who had once sold her soul to the Devil finds one who would buy that soul back. And one who was in the grip of hell, becomes the first to see a resurrected one. When we watch Jesus at work with Mary, we notice that there is no one who is beyond the reach of God's grace.

Throwing Stones
(The Adulterous Woman)

Certain sins seem to capture the limelight more than others, and adultery is surely one of them. As I write this very day, another very-high-profile athlete was caught in an "affair." There is something about sexual sins that heightens people's interest—and indignation. Perhaps it is the susceptibility we all have, and are unwilling to acknowledge, that makes us so judgmental.

Our Bibles include a footnote telling us that the story

of Jesus and the woman caught in adultery (John 7:53–8:11) is not in the oldest manuscripts of the gospel of John. Though it may not be from John's inspired pen, the depiction certainly bears all the marks of being just like Jesus. It illustrates not only Jesus' remarkable shrewdness in dealing with scoundrels, but more importantly His amazing grace in dealing with a "sinner." He is indeed the Master of wedding grace and truth in glorious balance, justice and mercy without compromising either, and law and due process in perfect equilibrium. Perhaps it is the imbalances that so often characterize us, and never Jesus, that both exude an odor the secular detect, and keep us from ministry that the secular would warm to.

Would the Real Prodigal Please Stand Up? (The Lost Son)

It is Jesus' association with "lost sheep" that evokes His most famous parable, the parable of the prodigal son, appropriately named "The Greatest Story Ever Told." Three important items are normally missed by the casual reader of Luke 15. One, the situation that elicits the parable is often overlooked, namely, Jesus' association with "sinners." Two, the text says, "Jesus told them this parable" (singular) and then Jesus launchs into the parable of the lost sheep, the lost coin, and the lost sons—one parable in three acts. It is likely that Jesus purposely contrasts the joy of finding a lost sheep and a lost coin with the outrageous lack of joy of finding a lost son. Three, though the main point of the parable in most circles today is the return of the "prodigal," the main point from Jesus' perspective is probably the behavior of the elder brother.

The brothers, both "sinners," are hardly recognized as such. One sees his father as a piggy bank, the other sees him as a slave driver. One is a hedonist, the other an egotist. One plays with the rules, the other thinks he's playing by the rules. One is rebellious, the other self-righteous. One's sins are overt, the other's are hidden. And the pain one experiences brings him to his senses and back home, and the other's "good life" is reinforced, causing him to stew in his juices and eventually reject grace.

Moreover, the contrast between the father and the older brother in their attitude and action toward the "prodigal" is stark. One is full of grace, the other can't get past fairness. One celebrates freely, the other refuses. One is Jesus and His followers, the other is the religious and theirs. When we watch Jesus at work with both "lost" and "found" we notice that He is never fooled by superficial righteousness, and never surprised by sin.

The "Godfather"
(Zacchaeus)

Matthew, one of Jesus' hand-selected disciples, is an

ordinary tax collector, and this is quite enough to vilify him in the minds of most Jews. But Zacchaeus, who we meet in Luke 19:1–10, is a big shot, the top dog in the taxation racket. The themes we have seen before in Jesus' interactions with the secular Jews are once again prominent here. Jesus takes the initiative, in this case telling the chief tax collector, "I must stay at your house today" (vv. 2, 5).

Zacchaeus and Jesus interact in a home setting. There is mutual respect, even admiration between them. Jesus' engagement with a known "sinner" is soundly criticized. And Jesus has a profound impact on Zacchaeus's life and destiny. It is Jesus' encounter with Zacchaeus that evokes the theme verses of the gospel of Luke, "Today salvation has come to this house, because this man, too, is a son of Abraham. For the Son of Man came to seek and to save what was lost" (vv. 9–10). When we watch Jesus at work among the disenfranchised, we notice that He often sees thirst when others see sin.

WALK WITH JESUS

Of all the groups Jesus interacted with, the secular Jews seemed to be among His favorites, and among the most fruitful. If the "heart and soul" of Judaism were the Sadducees and the Pharisees, then the secular Jews were way on the outside. Jesus sought them out and invited them in (or more accurately, invited Himself over). Jesus seemed to enjoy their company, and they His.

What was it about Jesus and the disenfranchised Jews that made them click? To start with, both were considered outsiders. Though Jesus perfectly kept the heart of the law, He did not follow some of the religious rules. So He was placed in the same soup with the sinners. Pariahs shared common treatment and emotions; they understood each other. Jesus must have loved the honesty many of the sinners displayed, and they must have loved the fact that He wasn't surprised by their sin. In the world of the first century, a man's home was his castle (and for the religious, his temple). So for Jesus to go to the homes of sinners and enjoy meals together was a clear statement of acceptance. Moreover, Jesus seemed to like the sinners and they liked Him; they seemed to enjoy life together. Jesus was completely natural and so were they. So when they compiled their guest list for parties, Jesus was on the list—how odd for a rabbi.

The ease with which Jesus interacted with the detached Jews does not mean that there weren't serious issues to discuss. Jesus did point out sin, where necessary and appropriate, but most of the time He didn't have to; they saw it themselves. Jesus never glamorized sin or participated in it, even though He freely interacted with those who did. Some secular Jews, as we have seen, seemed indifferent to Jesus, just as individuals from all of the other spiritual profiles also were. Apathy seems to be a universal, and dangerous, phenomenon.

A thread that runs through almost every encounter of Jesus with the lost sheep is money. Probably money was their substitute for God (cf. Matthew 6:24). It captured their affections, absorbed their time and energy, and gave them rewards—albeit temporal. In almost every encounter we find Jesus either addressing the money issue or the secular Jews addressing it. Matthew left his job and money to follow Jesus. The "sinful woman" and Mary Magdalene gave richly of their monies to Jesus and His disciples. One of the heart-hardening soils is one that is lured away from God by money. The "prodigal son" squandered his money, but pennilessness brought him to his senses. And Zacchaeus, perhaps the richest of all, demonstrated his newfound faith and faithfulness in monetary terms. Therefore, the grip of materialism is in all likelihood a seminal sin of the secular, the lost sheep. And generosity with money is a seminal sign that the grip has been broken.

How might Jesus interact with detached people today? Here are a dozen questions He might ask:

- Do you remember a time when church was a pleasant and rewarding experience? Do you miss it?
- Why have you walked away from "organized religion"?

- Are you guilty of "throwing the baby (Jesus) out with the bathwater (church)"? Have you generalized from a few to the many?
- What does it feel like to walk into a church? Do you miss it? What emotions well up within you? Or do you feel nothing?
- Do you harbor any residual bitterness from bad things that happened at church? How are you dealing with it?
- Do you ever feel proud that you are not like one of those churchgoing "hypocrites"?
- What kind of people would you never invite to a party at your house?
- What would be some of the qualities of a "religious person" that you would invite to your house for a party?
- Does a religious building or religious music ever give you a longing to know God?
- Do you see yourself as a sinner? How sensitive are you to your sin?
- How powerfully has money gripped your heart? Do you struggle with materialism?
- What compromises have you made to make more money?

WORK FOR JESUS

How might I be more useful in representing Jesus to people I meet who are religiously disenfranchised, detached from God and the church? Here are seven areas to consider as you interact with the detached.

1. Making a Connection

Jesus initiated most of the recorded interaction with the secular Jews and did so in the setting of a house over a meal. It is natural to simply write off those who have walked away from something you hold dear. However, this is not what Jesus did, nor should we do in His stead. Jesus knew, as we so easily forget, that those who have walked away generally have a reason (even if it is quite flimsy), feel like outcasts, are slightly embarrassed when they see us, and probably carry some residual guilt. They are often more spiritually sensitive than we think. Go to them, don't expect them to come to church. Accept them, even if they reject what you cherish. Have fun and be natural.

2. The Tone of the Conversation

"Almost playful" are the words I would choose to describe several of Jesus' encounters with the detached Jews. Jesus seemed to be the "life of the party," engaging in significant "table talk," among people who genuinely like each other. He was comfortable in dinner conversations with Matthew's tax-collecting friends, and apparently they were with him. When the teachers of the law criticized His eating with these "sinners," they probably overheard His tongue-in-cheek calling the Pharisee critics "righteous" and "healthy" (Mark 2:14–17). I once came across the anonymous quote, "Nowhere is there an account or portrait of Christ laughing . . . he is always stern, serious and as gloomy as a prison guard." I object! To the contrary, I cannot imagine a sought-after party guest who was not fun and laughed a lot.

I love pictures of Jesus laughing, and when I Google images of such, many appear on my computer screen. We will not represent Jesus well among people who feel disenfranchised from the religious institution if we are boring, judgmental, stiff, and uptight. These are probably among the reasons they abandoned church in the first place.

3. Finding Common Ground

Coupled with His outsider status, the food and fellowship certainly gave Jesus a lot of common ground with the detached Jews. Connecting at places of business, homes, and in public places also made for a sense of mutual comfort. Notice that for the most part Jesus did not say to the disenfranchised, "Come here," but rather He went there. Jesus doesn't quote Scripture to the secular Jews, but He does address sin. Sin is, in some ways, their language. So Jesus speaks it naturally, appropriately, graciously, and silently.

On a street corner in any city of the world ask the question, "Who do you think goes to heaven, the good or the bad?" and almost everyone will respond, "The good, of course!" That's the wrong answer from Jesus' perspective. When supposed "goodness" is the standard, common ground is replaced by competition. It is our profound understanding of brokenness that makes true the statement, "The ground is level at the foot of the cross."

4. Finding the Lost

Interestingly, it was in His conversation with Zacchaeus, a secular Jew, that Jesus declared His mission: "The Son of Man came to seek and to save what was lost" (Luke 19:10). Zacchaeus, though a Jew, probably had no sense of salvation. After all, he was a head honcho tax collector, a Roman collaborator, and a man who had gotten rich through graft. Surely, he would not have been on the elder board of the Jericho synagogue.

How did Jesus reach him? Zacchaeus' curiosity was met with Jesus' invitation. Zacchaeus' hospitality was met with Jesus' offer of God's hospitality in heaven. And Zacchaeus' offer to donate his possessions was met with Jesus' declaration that transformation had occurred. Now their dinner would be a celebration, rather than a mere social gathering.

5. Surprisingly . . .

Several things surprise me about Jesus' interactions with the secular Jews. First, I am surprised by how much He seemed to enjoy them, how at home He seemed to feel among them, and how relaxed they seemed to be around Jesus. I do not know of any so-called men of the cloth in my circle of friends who are on the top of the guest lists at the hottest parties in town! But Jesus was. Second, I am surprised that though almost every secular Jew with whom Jesus interacted had some connection with money, Jesus never brought up the subject—they did! Moreover, one of the telltale marks of their conversion was what they did with their money afterward.

I am also surprised by how important the detached Jews were to the kingdom once they became attached to Jesus. Matthew gave us a Gospel. The sinful woman gave us glimpses into the immensity of God's forgiveness. The down-cast tax collector shows us the prayer posture God loves. Zacchaeus shows us a model of the fruit of repentance. And Mary gave us the first look at the resurrected Jesus.

6. Slogans and Symbols

"Show Me the Money" the infamous slogan of the sports agent in *Jerry Maguire*, is a well-recognized line in popular culture today. Apparently, many of the disenfranchised have bought into the franchise of money. This makes sense because Jesus said that money was an alternative god (Matthew 6:24). In many cases, people have walked away from "organized religion" for financial reasons, and have substituted materialistic rewards in place of spiritual ones. As I reflect on people who I have known through the years who have walked away from church, they seem to have walked into an absorption with sports (especially the sports involvement of their children), work, recreation and leisure, partying, or even plain volunteering (a noble pursuit). Generally, a key indicator that God has captured their heart will also be reflected in their use of money.

7. Connecting with Jesus

The name most often associated with Jesus' interactions with the detached spiritual profile is simply "Jesus." I am sure this is not by accident. Jesus did not speak favorably about titles (Matthew 23:7–12). They tend to push people away rather than draw them close. With those who have removed themselves, or been removed, from the religious mainstream, titles are offensive, and tend to reinforce the very things the disenfranchised hate about the institution of religion. Knowing this, Jesus prefers to simply be who He is, and be called by His given name, just like them.

A pastor I know was asked during a congregational

meeting shortly after he assumed the pastorate of a church how he would like to be addressed. He had recently completed his Doctor of Ministry degree so he responded, "I prefer that you call me Dr. So-and-so." Several people who were present told me that that one comment was the beginning of the end for that pastor in that church. And sure enough, his tenure was very short and rough.

Remember George with whom I began this chapter? Though the money flowed, all did not go well with George. He started drinking too much and partying too hard. He overextended himself with business deals so that he could not pay his bills. Eventually he lost his wife, his kids, his job, his home, and was about to lose his life. My brother found him drinking himself to death in a cheap hotel room. And then George dropped out of our lives altogether.

Some ten years later, I had just finished a Sunday morning service and was greeting people at the door when a familiar face I could vaguely recognize walked up and shook my hand. It was George! He was sober and he looked good. He introduced me to his new wife and then told me that he had become a Christian and was faithfully involved in his church. And George said that my father, who had never walked away from him, was a big part in his coming to Christ.

Later, when I told my dad, he said he had heard about

George's conversion and was thrilled. But what I didn't know was what my father told me next. "Tom," he said, "every single month since George became a Christian he has sent me a small check to pay back what he squandered."

Profile:
The Samaritans

In general, the churches . . . bore for me the same relation to God that billboards did to Coca-Cola; they promoted thirst without quenching it.

—JOHN UPDIKE

3

JESUS *and the* SYNCRETISTS

When I encountered Zionists walking the red dirt roads of Africa in 1975, dressed in their long robes and carrying their prophetic staffs, I deliberately walked on the other side. As a westerner I understood the Zionists worshiped the ancestral spirits, so we intentionally distanced ourselves from them. Often late at night the rhythmic beating of their drums disturbed our sleep in the mission compound and their singing evoked existential fear. They were syncretists, fusing disparate religious beliefs and practices into a single religious expression. As spirit worshipers, heterodox in their beliefs, they were to be avoided at all costs.

The origins of these frightful syncretists began in 1904 when missionaries from the Christian Catholic Apostolic Church in Zion, Illinois, traveled to South Africa and evangelized the inhabitants. Four years later in 1908 these missionaries left abruptly. Now, one hundred years later, the seeds they sowed had blossomed into an indigenous religious force in the region called Zionism, comprising some 40 percent of all black South Africans!

Zionists fuse elements from the Old Testament (such as the taboo of eating pork and the acceptance of polygamy), with traditional African spiritism and worship (singing, dancing, clapping, and drumming), with some New Testament teachings (such as faith-healing and speaking in tongues), and added other culturally relevant religious expressions. Ancestor spirits plus the Holy Spirit, Judaism plus tribalism, biblical rituals with traditional dances, and priestly and prophetic symbols with shamanistic power—a potent, syncretistic mixture indeed!

Such were the Samaritans[1] of Jesus day. They fused religious ideas from various sources into a coherent indigenous religion. By most accounts the Samaritans were an ethnic mixture (Jewish, Assyrian, Canaanite), a religious mixture (monotheistic, polytheistic, pagan), and a scriptural mixture (Jewish Pentateuch and Samaritan Pentateuch). They combined teaching from the Old Testament, local culture and tradition, spirituality, and a deep emotional connection to the land to create a religion that made sense to them and gave them a deep sense of meaning. To the Jews of Jesus' day, the Samaritans were all mixed up. To Jesus they were spiritually ripe (John 4:34–38).

INTRODUCING
THE SAMARITANS

This religious blending and mixing by the Samaritans had deep historical roots. In 931 BC, Israel was ripped apart by civil war into northern and southern kingdoms. In the southern kingdom, Judah, was Jerusalem and its temple, center of Jewish worship. In the north, King Jeroboam I distracted his people by creating a blend of paganism and Judaism (1 Kings 12:25–33). The first mention of the region of Samaria in the Bible is a curse against its pagan syncretism (1 Kings 13:32).

Despite warnings and occasional token repentance, the people of the northern kingdom never adhered exclusively to Old Testament practices and lifestyle. By the time of Ahab and Jezebel, Baal worship had become Israel's religious norm and the prophets of God hid themselves in caves (1 Kings 16:29–22:40). And by 722 BC the northern kingdom was gone. The Assyrian army rolled over Samaria and the people vanished into exile, becoming the "ten lost tribes of Israel."

The new inhabitants (including a remnant of poor Jews) came from all over the Assyrian empire in order to settle and secure the land. They brought idols, sorcerers, and child sacrifice with them, and they mixed Old Testament religious practices with their native religion (2 Kings 17:24–41). Soon the Samaritans' syncretism was complete: "They worshiped the Lord, but they also served their own gods in accordance with the customs of the nations from which they had been brought" (2 Kings 17:33).

When the southern kingdom, Judah, was conquered and carried off to Babylon one hundred fifty years later, the Samaritans in the north continued to thrive. By the time the Jews began trickling back into Jerusalem, the Samaritans had been in place for almost two hundred years. Deciding who was "native" and who was "invader" depended on one's point of view. But from the perspective of the Jews, the Samaritans were racial and religious mongrels. When the Samaritans offered to help rebuild the Jerusalem temple, they were reviled as "enemies" by the Jews (Ezra 4:1–5). In response, the Samaritans subverted the building of the temple and city walls, and Jewish leaders, in turn, vigorously forbade intermarriage with Samaritans (Ezra 6; Nehemiah 13:23–28).

Jewish historian Josephus and the books of the Apocrypha fill in the chronicle of tension and animosity between Jew and Samaritan during the intertestamental period (ca.

433–5 BC). A few highlights trace the sordid story.

The Samaritans regarded Mount Gerizim as the site where Yahweh-worship began in the Promised Land (Genesis 12:6–8). In the fourth century BC, they built a temple there, and believed God's glory would return to it one day. Josephus says the Samaritans later dedicated the temple to the pagan god Jupiter. Whether this was the truth or Jewish propaganda isn't clear. In the end, the truth didn't matter. In 128 BC the Jews burned the Samaritan temple to the ground and Samaria surrendered to Jewish control in 109 BC.

In 63 BC the Romans came to "pacify" the region. Shortly before the birth of Jesus, Samaritans scattered human bones in the temple in Jerusalem, defiling it during the Passover.[2] John the apostle's statement, "the Jews have nothing to do with the Samaritans" summed up the situation.

Bad blood over centuries solidified between the Jews and the Samaritans. The Jews developed an attitude of racial, cultural, and religious superiority. The Samaritans nursed their roles as outcasts, martyrs, and victims. The two peoples simply kept their distance. By the time of Christ, Jews bypassed Samaria when traveling between Judea and Galilee even though such a detour was costly— time and money pale compared to prejudice. The writings of the period are saturated with vitriol: "He that eats the bread of the Samaritans is like to one that eats the flesh of swine."[3] Those "who live on the mountains of Samaria," are "no nation," including "the foolish people that live in Shechem."[4] To a Jew, "Samaritan" was a cuss word (John 8:48). The virulent hatred between Jews and Samaritans involved race, religion, geography, history, literature, even the afterlife! As Bible scholar Kenneth Bailey reminds us, "Heretics and schismatics are usually despised more than unbelievers."[5]

The plight of the Samaritans since Jesus' day has been mixed. They experienced great suffering at the hands of Pilate and received severe treatment during the Jewish Revolt (AD 66–73). After the revolt, the Samaritans were allowed to rebuild their temple and remain in the land. Though almost twenty centuries have passed since the last mention of the Samaritans in the Bible, a small remnant of Samaritans still reside in Nablus (Shechem) in the West Bank.

TENDENCIES of the Samaritans

T*ruth:* The Samaritan's edition of the Scriptures was called the Samaritan Pentateuch. Their compilation of the books of Moses altered the Tenth Commandment to require the worship of God to occur inside Samaria on Mt. Gerizim, and they named themselves the "Observant Ones." They rejected the remainder of the Old Testament and other Jewish writings.

E*conomics:* Without specific mention of the Samaritan's economic and social status, we assume them to be working class farmers, artisans, and traders. Certainly there were poor Samaritans (like the leper in Luke 17) and wealthier Samaritans (like the "Good Samaritan" in Luke 10).

N*eighborhood:* The Samaritans had few outside friends. The Jews considered them outcasts and the Romans branded them a regional Jewish cult. Yet outcasts often bond with a strong sense of community. The "Observant Ones" considered themselves true believers defined in opposition to the infidel Jews and Roman pagans.

D*evotion:* Samaritans followed the Mosaic law, including circumcision, Sabbath keeping, and kosher living. True worship at the true sanctuary following the true law of God was the way to truly please God. The Samaritans looked for a "Taheb" or "Restorer" to come and set things right. As the Jews saw the coming Messiah primarily in political terms, the Samaritans saw the "Taheb" primarily in prophetic terms. As the Jews looked forward to a righteous king, the Samaritans looked for a Teacher like Moses (Deuteronomy 18:15–19).

E*veryman:* Little is known about the Samaritans' view of human beings. We can assume that they considered human nature morally neutral, sin a choice, and atonement and restoration a necessity.

N*ature of God:* The Samaritans saw themselves as the true worshipers of the one true God of Israel. The Jews, on the other hand, viewed the Samaritans as polytheists and syncretists. At the time of Jesus, the Samaritans' view of God ironically was similar to the view of the Jews; they disagreed over small aspects of how Yahweh should be worshiped. However, a huge disagreement separated them regarding the location for that worship.

Civics: The Samaritans were caught between opposing forces geographically and politically. To their south lay Jerusalem and the hated Jews. On their northern border was "Galilee of the Gentiles." Generally the Samaritans leaned more toward the Roman government with whom they usually collaborated in order to keep the peace and enjoy a measure of prosperity.

Immortality: The Samaritans believed in a resurrection followed by final judgment. Those judged righteous would live in the garden of Eden and condemned persons would burn.

Ethics: The Mosaic law provided the source for Samaritan ethics and the basis for all moral choice.

Summary: Through centuries of mixing with peoples around them, the Samaritans became pious syncretists. Their ethnic roots were mixed. Their geography was mixed. Their worship was a mixture of religious features. The Samaritans were mixed—and the Jews would have added with gusto "mixed up!"

WATCH JESUS

How did Jesus interact with the Samaritans in His day? Consider these six encounters.

A Most Unlikely Encounter
(The Woman at the Well)

If ever there was an unlikely encounter in the ministry of Jesus it was with the Samaritan woman recorded in John 4:1–42. A host of factors could or should have nixed the entire event. Nevertheless, this encounter constitutes one of the longest recorded conversations Jesus had with an individual in the Gospels. This alone should give us good reason to consider it carefully. When we watch Jesus at work we notice that He goes where "angels fear to tread."

Artificial human barriers never limit Jesus. The classic account of the woman at Jacob's well shows Him breaching many of them. One, Jesus breaks the barrier of avoidance. We read, "Now he had to go through Samaria" (v. 4). Other Jews take an inconvenient and circuitous route simply to avoid the Samaritans. Not Jesus. Two, He defies the barrier of racial prejudice as the Jews and the Samaritans mutually vilify each other (v. 9). Three, He cracks the barrier of gender (vv. 9, 27). The societal strictures against gender mixing were formidable in Jesus' day, as they are in strict Muslim countries today. Four, He violates the barrier of self-help by asking an unlikely stranger for a favor. Five, He transgresses the barrier of defilement by asking to use a soiled Samaritan bucket. Six, Jesus contravenes the barrier of social propriety by interacting with a woman known to have a sordid past and even prying into her love life (vv. 16–18). Seven, He destroys the barrier of religion by ultimately declaring all temples obsolete (vv. 19–24). Eight, He breaches multiplied historical barriers by putting centuries of suspicion and conflict to rest. And lastly, Jesus bursts the barrier of salvation timing, declaring the harvest to be coincident with the planting (vv. 35–42).

Not only does Jesus overcome the barriers to reach the Samaritans, He also replaces those barriers with bridges. He intentionally invades space that others avoid. He takes initiative. He humbles Himself by asking for a favor. He ignores distancing taboos. He "risks" defilement. He stimulates thirst and then offers to quench it. He chooses to live in the present, not the past. He decides to ignore her past with just a passing comment. He engages a Samaritan woman with many strikes against her in significant spiritual conversation. And Jesus masterfully prompts her to consider who He is—the ultimate question.

Jesus' identity becomes the primary issue in the conversation between the two. Notice the progression of this Samaritan woman's understanding of Jesus: a thirsty man (v. 7), a Jew (v. 9), an exaggerator (v. 11), a fellow child of

Jacob (v. 12), a magician (v. 15), a prophet (v. 19), a priest (vv. 21–24), the Messiah (vv. 25–26), "I Am" (v. 26), the Savior of the world (v. 42). When we watch Jesus at work with the Samaritan woman we notice that He resists the temptation to engage the woman in religious debate and demonstrate her error. Instead He keeps the primary focus primary—Himself!

The quest of the woman at Jacob's well is common to all. She is looking for love. She must not have found it socially or she wouldn't have come to the well alone in the heat of the day. She may have found it, perversely, in her underdog status. She seemed to have found it, distantly, in her connection with a famous ancestor. She ventured to find it, temporarily, with a string of men. She seemed to have found it, superficially, in her Mount Gerizim religion. And then she found it— eternally, in relationship with the Savior of the world!

Slow to Take Offense
(The Inhospitable Samaritans)

People who are marginalized are often hypersensitive to slights. This seemed to be true among the Samaritans. At the outset of His ministry, Jesus made friends among the Samaritans. So it was likely expected that Jesus would pay His respects whenever He made His way through Samaritan country. After all, hospitality is a supreme virtue in that part of the world.

Luke records (9:51–56) that Jesus is on His way to Jerusalem and decides to take the quickest route through Samaria. As is His practice, Jesus sends out an advance group to arrange accommodations. However, the Samaritans stonewall the preparations because the pilgrims are Jews going to a Feast. James and John, the "Sons of Thunder" (Mark 3:17), want to play Elijah and call down fire from heaven (2 Kings 1:9–16) on the uncooperative Samaritans. Jesus, however, rebukes his impetuous disciples, ignores the Samaritan slight, and uses the incident to teach His disciples about the cost of following Him.

Rejection easily breeds rejection, which breeds rejection, and the beat goes on! Jesus taught His disciples that rejection is an inevitable part of discipleship, but responding in kind is not appropriate (cf. 2 Peter 3:9). Jesus opted for a better response to rejection—sadness (Luke 19:41–44). When we watch Jesus at work among the Samaritans we notice that He is slow to take offense even when provoked. We need not be offended or even angered when the mixed religionist rejects us.

The S Word
(The Cursed Samaritans)

In John 7–8 Jesus is at the Feast of Tabernacles in Jerusalem. The opposition from the religious leaders now becomes intense. Ten references are made in these chapters to the opposition's desire to harm Jesus.[6] As Jesus asserts His messianic credentials, and the people wrestle with His assertions, the religious leaders push back with denials, derogatory comments, and procedural rabbit trails; they even attempt to arrest Him. In response, Jesus refuses to back away from the fray. Instead He becomes more pointed in His comments. Jesus informed the religious leaders that they were not truly Abraham's children, instead they were children of the Devil.

Utterly exasperated with the impertinent false rabbi from Galilee, the Jewish religious leaders dig deep into their repertoire of horrible names and come up with the worst possible cuss combination: "Aren't we right in saying that you are a Samaritan and demon-possessed?" (8:48). Interestingly, Jesus counters the "demon-possessed" accusation, but lets the "Samaritan" epithet stand. When we watch Jesus at work among His own people, we notice that He is not afraid to identify with "the enemy."

Good Muslim Jihadist?
(The Good Samaritan)

What comes to mind today when you hear the word "Samaritan"? I suspect some of the following: the parable of the good Samaritan, Good Samaritan hospitals, Good Samaritan laws, Samaritan's Purse, the Good Samaritan Society. Did you notice that every connection with the word "Samaritan" is overwhelmingly positive? Today's perspective of "Samaritans" is the polar opposite of the Jewish perspective in Jesus' day. In Jesus' day the Samaritans were the scum of the earth.

To attempt to mirror the antipathy, antagonism, and downright hatred associated with Samaritans in the first century, we might suggest terms like "skin head" or "Muslim jihadist" or "radical communist." To a Jew of Jesus' day, there was no one on the face of the earth as bad as a Samaritan. Now Jesus audaciously tells one of His most famous stories about a "good Samaritan" (Luke 10:25–37). He makes a hated Samaritan the overwhelming hero of the story and the Jewish religionists the goats. It is even possible that the story of the good Samaritan recounts an actual event.

In June 2000, I traveled to Damascus, Syria. One evening we were invited to the home of a poor family who demonstrated amazingly rich hospitality. They emptied their pocketbook to rent a van to transport us. They filled their house with friends to welcome us. They filled our stomachs with treats to feed us. They invited musicians to entertain us. And finally (at 2 a.m.!) they sent us on our way with gift bags to honor us. None of us ever experienced such warm hospitality before or since—and these people were complete strangers. Syria is regarded in our part of the world as a terrorist-sponsoring nation. And, obviously, the country is overwhelmingly Muslim. Nevertheless, while I disagree with many of the tenets of Islam, I could find no flaw in the hospitality and sincere kindness we were shown in Damascus.

So, I could tell a story about a "good Shiite from Syria" that puts the hospitality of all Christians I know to utter shame. Now, normally we would be reluctant to tell such stories as they make Christians look bad and Muslims look good. But Jesus doesn't do the "normal" thing. He courageously highlights the positives in persons uniformly considered bad and exposes the negatives in those often thought to be good.

What is Jesus doing through this parable? Perhaps He is building bridges. Perhaps He is seeking common ground. Perhaps He is sabotaging barriers. Or perhaps He is simply telling the truth. Jesus doesn't have an axe to grind, a system to defend or demolish, or a religion to fear. But He does have a person to love—a syncretic, mixed-up Samaritan who wants to know God.

I am aware of a thriving Conservative Baptist Church in Utah that has built bridges to reach the local culture with the gospel. Among the keys to the effectiveness of their outreach is a refusal to accept an "us-against-them" mentality, and a prohibition against put-downs. Like Jesus at work among the Samaritans, they are unafraid to acknowledge genuine goodness among those widely considered heretical.

Uncommon Gratitude

(The Thankful Samaritan)

Jesus is on His way from Galilee to Jerusalem for the last time before He is crucified. On the border between Galilee and Samaria ten lepers shout out to Jesus for pity from a therapeutic distance (Luke 17:11–19). Jesus shouts back that they should go to the medical examiner, the priest, and obtain official certification of their healing. The text reveals that both Jews and Samaritans comprise the group of untouchables (misery demolishes traditional barriers). But Luke tells us the "rest of the story." Only one returns to say thanks, and he was a Samaritan! Once again the Bible highlights the goodness of the "bad."

Why does Dr. Luke tell us that a lone Samaritan returns to thank Jesus? Perhaps God wanted to highlight the paucity of gratitude. Undoubtedly, it would have been more politically correct to conveniently leave out that incendiary tidbit. Obviously, a good reason to include it was because it happened and it was true. But is there more? Perhaps it was included as a polemic against the Jews. Perhaps it was included as a precursor to Luke's mention of the gospel reaching the Samaritans. Or perhaps he included it simply to say something good about a group of people that few Jews said anything good about.

Once again Jesus is building bridges. When we watch

Jesus at work, we notice that He is the ultimate objective, a rare trait among people in general.

The Samaritan Pentecost
(The Spirit of Jesus and the Samaritan Church)

Shortly after Jesus ascended, the Holy Spirit descended, and Stephen was martyred, Philip brought the gospel to the Samaritans, and many responded (Acts 8:4–8). Ironically one of those who once wanted to call down "fire from heaven" to destroy some Samaritans (Luke 9:54) now confirms the conversion of the Samaritans (Acts 8:14–17).

Interest in things spiritual is evident in all the accounts of the gospel going to the Samaritans. Evil spirits (v. 7), the spirit of sorcery (vv. 9–25), and the Holy Spirit all show up prominently in the text of Acts 8. Syncretism and spirituality, two of the common identifying markers of the Samaritans, are like cousins. Some of the Samaritans were apparently demonized and others, like Simon, were caught up in sorcery. Their spirituality caused them to seek out and acquire the power of spiritual sources most orthodox believers would shun. The followers of Jesus, now indwelt by the Spirit of Jesus, however, marched unafraid into syncretistic Samaritan country.

Spiritualism is on the rise in America (even as "organized religion" is declining).[7] In spite of decades of materialist indoctrination, people seem to be incorrigibly spiritual. They actively pursue a connection with a reality beyond the physical world. People seem to recognize the reality of spirits and energy outside the realm of the senses. People seek, and often find, means to connect with the realm of the spirit through practices such as meditation, chanting, asceticism, silence, mysticism, horoscopes, and the occult.

People seek a subjective encounter with a power source beyond themselves, or deep within themselves. People thirst for an encounter with the divine, to tap the power of the unseen. Spirituality, in a variety of forms, is apparently common among the syncretists. Those seeking to interact with spiritual syncretists will have to wade into the uncomfortable waters of nonbiblical spirituality. Most orthodox believers would rather flee than reach out to those who interact with "other" spiritual sources.

How did Jesus' ambassadors interact in Acts 8 with people who were into syncretistic spirituality? First, they knew the truth so well that error was apparent (Acts 2:42). Then they confronted it (8:7), they countered it with the good news (v. 12), they replaced it with a greater power, the Holy Spirit (vv. 15–17), they exposed spiritual counterfeits (vv. 18–23), and they preached God's Word (v. 25).

The last record of the Samaritans in the Bible is most encouraging. In Acts 9:31 we read that the church in Samaria "enjoyed a time of peace. It was strengthened; and encouraged by the Holy Spirit, it grew in numbers, living in the fear of the Lord." And Acts 15:3 assumes a thriving Christian church among the Samaritans. The barriers Jesus breached blossomed into a rich harvest and the bridges He built brought eternal results (John 4:35–38).

WALK WITH JESUS

Of all the spiritual profiles with whom Jesus interacted, the Samaritans seemed to be ones of whom He spoke most positively. Jesus found a lot to like in the Samaritans. First, He had a tender heart for the underdog. While His fellow Jews would run, shun, and make fun of the Samaritans, Jesus chose to engage them intentionally. Second, Jesus (and later His disciples) discovered the Samaritans to be particularly open to Him and the gospel. The Samaritans were the first group of people (prior to the disciples or the Jews) who believed (John 4:39). And then the Samaritans were the first group (after the Jews in Jerusalem) who responded to the gospel after Pentecost. Third, the Samaritans (at least individuals among them) embodied some highly commendable traits including: spiritual curiosity (John 4), good deeds (Luke 10), and gratitude (Luke 17).

Jesus also recognized the Samaritans to be genuinely warm toward those who were warm to them. Though initially suspicious, the Samaritans grew to trust Jesus (and later His followers). Finally, Jesus recognized the Samaritans knew that things were not as they were intended to be, and thus looked for a "Restorer"—and found One in Jesus!

Still, the Samaritans embodied flaws that are present with many mixed-up worshipers. There was the Samaritans' search for spiritual meaning—intense yet incautious (as Acts tells us). Jesus acknowledged the reality of this thirst, but both He and His apostles pointed out that this thirst had led them down spiritually dangerous and dead-end paths. The Samaritan woman's thirst led her to a multiplicity of men. The Samaritan people's thirst for acceptance caused them to exaggerate slights. The Samaritan people's thirst for supernatural power caused them to be overly impressed with disreputable people like Simon the sorcerer, and entrapped by demons themselves.

Jesus did not hesitate to point out sin and error to the Samaritans. For example, to the woman at the well He pointed out her sexual indiscretion and her theological error ("salvation is from the Jews," John 4:22), but He didn't dwell on it.

If Jesus could spend an afternoon walking and talking with Samaritan-like people today, I suspect He might approach them like He did the Samaritans He met many years ago. Here are several questions He might ask:

- Has anyone whose worldview clashes with yours ever shown you unexpected kindness? If so, how did you respond?
- What barriers have you built that keep people who don't believe as you do outside your life? Why?
- Has your thirst been quenched by the spiritual system you have fused together? Do you live with much internal dissonance trying to combine different spiritual strains into a cohesive worldview?
- Has the neglect of the religious mainstream made you more brazen or more broken?
- How do you react when your genuine offers of help are rebuffed? How does it feel to be rejected by those who hold dissimilar religious views?
- What standard do you employ to discern what is true and what is not? Why is your standard superior to others?
- How has being considered an outcast affected the way you view yourself? How have you responded?
- Has your performance of good deeds drawn you closer or made you more distant from God? Have good works worked for you?
- How has gratitude opened up your heart to God?
- What kind of "Messiah" do you long for? Where are you on the path of discovering who Jesus is?

WORK FOR JESUS

How might you be more useful and effective in representing Jesus to people you meet who are Samaritan in background and outlook? Here are seven areas to consider as you interact with the syncretists who blend beliefs.

1. Making a Connection

In our world, "Samaritans" are everywhere! The Samaritan spiritual profile pervades American culture as part of our melting pot of ethnicities, religions, and worldviews. Individualism, pluralism, choice, and tolerance are among our most cherished values. Many Americans believe they have the right to individualize their belief system, to select from a variety of options.

In Jesus' day the Samaritans were isolated, today they live next door. Nevertheless, going next door is sometimes as formidable a challenge as traveling through Samaria was in Jesus' day. The main way Jesus made a connection with the syncretistic Samaritans was to purposely choose not to avoid them and intentionally choose to engage them. Among His approaches, He initiated interactions with them, asked for favors and ignored rejection from them, and pointed out goodness in them. What a good pattern to follow.

2. The Tone of the Conversation

When Jesus interacted with the Samaritans He seemed to be constantly inviting them into relationship with Himself. The biblical word that summarizes this tone is "hospitality" or a "love of strangers."[8] If we are going to represent Jesus, we must develop a love for people different from us, even—or especially—those who hold dissimilar spiritual beliefs. How does one set an inviting tone with syncretists? Don't avoid them, marginalize them, malign them, or prejudge them. Instead, engage them, commend them (where appropriate), correct them (where appropriate), and focus on pointing them to Jesus. He is the main thing.

3. Finding Common Ground

The common ground Jesus shared with the Samaritans was His outsider status. From His birth onward, Jesus was the quintessential outsider. His own did not understand, recognize, or receive Him (John 1:5, 10–11). He was called derogatory names. Whisperings about His birth and parentage lingered throughout His life. Jesus did not attend the "right" schools or travel in the "right" circles or select the "right" friends. He could genuinely feel the Samaritans' pain.

Painful slights, slurs, and strikes indeed do hurt. But they also mold us. And if we let God use them for good, He will, forging common ground with those who experience similar pains. Having personally had a child with cancer has given me some common ground to connect with other families going through similar trials.

4. Losing the Found

The Samaritans, as represented by the Samaritan woman, thought that they got it right when it came to religion. They thought they had found true religion. They believed their interpretation of the Holy Books was right, their holy mountain was the right one, and their pursuit of the Restorer was also right. Refusing to "rub it in," Jesus straightforwardly affirmed that the Jews (not the Samaritans) "have it right," and yet the Jews too have missed the point. God is not so much interested in "rightness" as in righteousness, not so much interested in where we worship but who. Jesus didn't hesitate to point out sin, but seemed to dwell more on unfulfilled longings. This approach produces both brokenness and hope.

It has been said that there are two ways to get to a person's heart: by pointing out their sin, or by appealing to their deep longings. We usually opt for the first and ignore the thirst (Psalm 42:1–2). The impression I get both from the Samaritans historically and syncretists in my own sphere of life is one of unquenched thirst for acceptance and love. Offering a "drink" is often more effective than exposing error, and encouraging their spirit is more effective than exposing the spirits. I wonder where today's "wells" are located? Probably we'd find Jesus there!

5. Surprisingly . . .

I was shocked when I first realized that the group of people Jews in Jesus' day had nothing good to say about were the very group that Jesus says the most good about. Of all the spiritual profiles Jesus interacted with, none received more accolades than the Samaritans! The Samaritan woman, though having lived a "bad" life, has a huge impact for good on her fellow villagers. Stunningly, Jesus tells a parable about a "Good" Samaritan. When Jesus heals ten lepers, only one—a Samaritan—expressed his gratitude. And the first group to embrace the Good News outside of Judaism were the Samaritans.

Jesus was a genius at human relations. He knew that to focus on negative things with a group that already feels like outcasts (or martyrs) will only push them deeper into their false religion. Genuinely highlighting the good things they do opens ears and hearts. We, like Jesus, must not overlook the virtues of people who subscribe to various religious mixtures. These good things may well be the bridge to their soul. Jesus was not reluctant to hold them up to praise. We may be surprised to find that virtue and compassion lurk in the strangest places.

Why are we so reluctant to see and praise the acts of

goodness of those with whom we disagree theologically? Are we afraid they'll show us up? What's new? Are we concerned lest we give support and encouragement to their belief system? We must leave that to God. Are we religiously envious or fearful? Isn't He greater (1 John 4:4)? Jesus didn't seem to be hesitant in the least to highlight Samaritan goodness and gratitude, two very lofty virtues.

6. Slogans and Symbols

Water figures prominently in Jesus' interactions with the Samaritans. Jesus met the Samaritan woman at a well, asked for a drink of water, and offered living water. The Feast of Tabernacles, to which Jesus was heading when He encountered the Samaritans, and the Feast where He was called a "Samaritan" involved significant water symbolism. Surely the "Good Samaritan" used some of his water to care for the battered man on the road. And when the Samaritans embraced the gospel they were duly baptized in water. For the Samaritans, thirst depicts the state of their souls—desperately seeking without soul satisfaction (Jeremiah 2:13). The outpouring of water symbolizes the Spirit that would transform their lives (Isaiah 44:3–4; John 4:10). Water is also a symbol of the joy of their salvation (Isaiah 12:3). What a difference it makes when we interact with people whose belief system, and likely also their life, is all mixed up if we approach them on the level of their thirst rather than the level of their sin. Sprite advertises "Obey Your Thirst." We should remember to "Convey Our Thirst."

7. Connecting with Jesus

The ultimate question Jesus wanted every spiritual profile to wrestle with was His identity and the implications thereof. And the way Jesus presented Himself to each spiritual profile was uniquely fitting. The Samaritans had been primed by their history, Scriptures, culture, and mistreatment to long for a Messiah-Restorer. Jesus invitingly revealed Himself to them.

"The main thing is to keep the main thing the main thing."[9] Though this oft-quoted statement sounds like double-talk, it is profound and practical. One of the great dangers in working for Jesus with Samaritan-like people is that we will get sidetracked by tangential—and irritating—issues on which we disagree. Jesus could have debated the Samaritans' ethnic and religious roots. Jesus could have debunked their version of the Scriptures. Jesus could have commiserated with the Samaritans over the poor press they received from the Jews. Jesus could have discussed ad nauseam their historical conflicts with the Jews. Jesus could have engaged in a lengthy theological discussion with the Samaritan woman over holy mountains. But He didn't! Instead Jesus kept the main thing the main thing—Himself!

Remember, people are incorrigibly spiritual; they often

seek reality beyond the physical world. When you meet those whose religion comes mixed—perhaps some mysticism and meditation, with a dash of the Scriptures—know that their real thirst is for an encounter with the divine. Like the Samaritan woman at the well, they seek truth. Point them to Jesus. Especially His words that day that those who would worship God must do so "in spirit and in truth," and His declaration, "I . . . am he [the Christ]" (John 4:23–26), the one sent from God for spiritual salvation.

Profile:
The Sadducees

You can safely assume that you've created God in your own image when it turns out that God hates all the same people you do.

—ANNE LAMOTT

4

JESUS *and the* TRADITIONALISTS

There are certain people we love to hate—particularly those who are powerful and successful. Ironically we loathe them and are fascinated by them at the same time. We follow their every move on TV and in magazines. We hang on their words and sometimes hang on their fashion tastes. We deeply believe that if we were in their shoes we would walk differently. And we secretly wish we could trade places with them.

People generally love to hate those on top. Those, who by virtue of their birth, appearance, wealth, power, position, or education, have "made it," are regularly reviled . . . and secretly admired; caricatured and copied; detested and desired; mocked and mirrored.

In Jesus' day the group of people that everyone loved to hate were the Sadducees.[1] They were rich, powerful, and successful. They were the small group that everyone fumed against—and fawned over. They were the Jewish "top-dogs" culturally, politically, and religiously. If they lived in our world they would attract the paparazzi, give their erudite opinions on news shows, live in nice houses, and roam the corridors of power. The Sadducees were inarguably the best educated of the eight groups of people with whom Jesus interacted. The Sadducees controlled the temple in Jerusalem, ran the religious bureaucracy, dominated the Sanhedrin, performed a host of administrative functions, and ran interference with the Romans. They were the power people of their day.

INTRODUCING
THE SADDUCEES

The Sadducees emerged as an identifiable group during the intertestamental period (the approximately four hundred years between the writing of Malachi and Matthew). During this period, Alexander the Great (356–323 BC) cast a long political and cultural shadow on the people and land of Israel. As a result, some Jews in Israel spoke the Greek language and embraced a Greek worldview. Others vehemently opposed Hellenism, eventually resulting in the

Maccabean Revolt (167–164 BC). In this revolt the Jewish people succeeded in overthrowing the Hellenists and established a new (non-Davidic) Jewish dynasty called the Hasmoneans (166–63 BC). Under this dynasty of Jewish rulers, the offices of high priest, military commander, and king were combined.

The Sadducees are identified as a group for the first time in the writings of Josephus during the reign of the Hasmonean king John Hyrcanus (134–104 BC). No mention is made of their origins, so we are left to speculate. Clearly, the religious and political intrigue of the Hasmonean Dynasty created the conditions that gave rise to the Sadducees, and their opponents, the Pharisees and the Essenes.

Although the Jewish people secured their independence from the Hellenists, Hellenism did not go away. Ironically, the very dynasty that ousted the Hellenists came to embrace Hellenism! This led to a major rift among the religious leaders of Israel with some opposing Hellenism (they became the Pharisees) and others embracing it (they became the Sadducees). Various Hasmonean monarchs favored one party or the other, with the Sadducees generally having a closer tie with the powers that be.

Jewish independence came to an end when, weakened by infighting among the Hasmoneans, the Romans under Pompey conquered Jerusalem in 63 BC. When Herod the

Great (37–4 BC) assumed control over the governance of Israel, the aristocratic Sadducees maintained a shaky collaboration with the Roman government thus preserving their wealth and a measure of power. During the time of Jesus, they dominated the temple and the Sanhedrin while the Pharisees controlled the synagogues.

TENDENCIES of the Sadducees

Truth: The Sadducees recognized only the law of Moses (Genesis through Deuteronomy) as the source of divine truth. They respected the rest of the Old Testament, but not as a source of law, and they vehemently rejected the oral law of the Pharisees (the Mishnah). Moreover, the Sadducees did not believe in the supernatural, thus stripping even their pared-down Bible of its miracles. Thus, the Sadducees' source of truth eventually became a hybrid of Mosaic morals and rituals and humanistic applications.

Economics: The Sadducees were decidedly upper class. And with their wealth came education, connections, and power. Moreover, since the Sadducees believed earthly existence was all there was, they determined to "live richly"—and they did.

Neighborhood: The Sadducees were generally acknowledged as the official leaders of the Jewish community. As such they were respected, even if not admired. Among each other, however, Josephus remarks, "The behaviour of the Sadducees one towards another is in some degree wild; and their conversation with those that are of their own party is as barbarous as if they were strangers to them."[2] Perhaps the cauldron of competition in which they operated stripped away a measure of common courtesy.

Devotion: The Sadducees' understanding of the spiritual life was a combination of sacred and secular. They believed that the things of God should be revered, yet not restrictively. They sought a good life on earth and viewed God's law, the temple, and religious ritual as a means to that good life. The Sadducees essentially were materialists, denying the spirit world. They placed no trust in angels to help them or demons to tempt them.

Everyman: The Sadducees were humanists. They believed that human beings are rational and have free choice. The human soul was essentially good. And since this world was all there was, their goal was to make life as good as possible for themselves—and others.

Nature of God: The Sadducees were functional Deists. They believed in God, but not a God who is active in human affairs. They believed in divine law, but not in divine involvement. They believed in the temple liturgy and religious tradition as a means of making life better in the hereand-now, not the hereafter. They believed in the rituals of

God but not a relationship with God. Thus, God was important to life, but at best distant and temporal.

Civics: The Sadducees may well have coined the sentence, "When ruled by Rome, do as the Romans do." Of all of the religious groups in Israel in the time of Jesus, the Sadducees were the most accommodating to the Romans—for the mutual benefit of both. The Romans gave the Sadducees a measure of power and the Sadducees delivered to the Romans a measure of peace and order. They were the peacekeepers and the power brokers who generally used their position capably. And the Sadducees profited handsomely from this arrangement financially and politically.

Immortality: Perhaps you have heard the line, "The Sadducees did not believe in the resurrection, that is why they were sad, you see." Whether sadness dominated their emotional state or not we do not know, but it is true that they did not believe in an afterlife; when the body died so did the soul. According to the Sadducees there was no future resurrection, no rewards for the righteous or punishment for the evil. The best that could be hoped for was a good life in this world both individually and for the nation. And the Sadducees worked to provide both.

Ethics: The Sadducees' ethics combined God's (natural) laws with pragmatic concerns. On one hand, the Sadducees were sticklers for the letter of the law, particularly in matters of justice. On the other hand, the Sadducees were progressives in the sense that they interpreted the law in light of changing times. Thus, they were more tolerant on matters such as marriage and sex.

S*ummary:* Merriam-Webster's New Collegiate Dictionary defines power as the "possession of control, authority, or influence over others." Clearly, the Sadducees possessed (and some were possessed by) power. Their position of power combined conveniently with their theology. Their belief system emphasized human control of life on earth based on God's laws.

WATCH JESUS

How did Jesus interact with the Sadducees in His day? Consider these nine encounters.

Attention Grabber

(The Keepers of the Temple)

Jesus' first encounter with the Sadducees is epic (John 2:13–25). Though the Sadducees are not mentioned specifically, clearly John's "the Jews" (vv. 18, 20) refers primarily to them. Since it is Passover, the Sadducees are front and center, prominent and proud, in Jerusalem. The great Jewish feasts are the Sadducees' opportunity to shine. They control the personnel, mechanics, and ministries of the temple.

Jesus stunningly disrupts the show. He invades the Sadducees' turf, rejects what they have allowed, and calls their domain His house! Messing with the temple is tantamount to picking a fight with the Sadducees. And pick a fight Jesus does! He literally knocks down some tables, asserts His ownership of the "House," jabs at the Sadducees' disbelief in the resurrection, and pummels their mismanagement of the temple. Appropriately, the Sadducees demand Jesus' credentials. Bafflingly, Jesus presents exhibit one, *His* temple, i.e., His body (vv. 18–20).

So Jesus initiates a relationship with the Sadducees with an attention-grabber. He mounts a frontal assault on their power base. Perhaps Jesus is serving notice to the power elite that an alternative "power source" has arrived. Perhaps Jesus is seeking to shock the Sadducees out of the status quo. Perhaps Jesus is lovingly smashing some of their traditional idols. Or maybe Jesus is simply speaking their language—power. When we watch Jesus at work among the Sadducees, we notice that He speaks the language of power among the powerful.

Sign Blind
(The Sign-Seeking Sadducees)

Every teacher has had students who "ask" questions with ulterior motives. Some desire to show up the teacher, and others to show off their knowledge. Jesus, the master teacher, faces such a question from the Sadducees (and the Pharisees—strange bedfellows indeed!) when He is "asked" for some authenticating miracle to substantiate His claims (Matthew 16:1–12). Jesus characteristically cuts to the heart of the matter. He highlights the anomaly of their being able to accurately predict signs in the skies (natural phenomena) but unable to see signs of the times (spiritual perception). Jesus then chastises the religious leaders for seeking signs as a substitute for seeking God. Finally, Jesus offers the ultimate sign, the "sign of Jonah" (v. 4), a reference to His resurrection. Ironically, the Sadducees do not even believe in signs, or resurrection!

When we watch Jesus at work among the Sadducees, we notice that He is both direct and elusive. He directly confronts their inability to ascertain the meaning of signs, and then elusively offers the "sign of Jonah." Apparently the Sadducees are not curious enough to follow up.

Benign Neglect
(The Shunned Sadducees)

Sometimes the most loving thing one can do is to ignore someone. When a child is throwing a tantrum, often the most loving response is to simply ignore their inappropriate means of seeking attention. When a student is disrupting a classroom with incessant questions, the most loving response may be to ignore them. And when people are cocksure of their own self-importance, the best way to love them may be to ignore them. Benign neglect is sometimes the most loving thing to do. The most unloving thing to do is to feed their ego.

Interestingly, the account of the Sadducees asking Jesus for a sign is the *only* recorded interaction with the Sadducees between Jesus' first temple cleansing (at the outset of His public ministry) and the last few weeks of His life. Reading between the lines one can detect several times Jesus indirectly mentions the Sadducees (as in Matthew 16:21; Mark 8:31; 10:33–34 where Jesus predicts His sufferings at the hands of the "chief priests") or when Jesus may have had superficial contact with them (as in Matthew 17:24–27, when Jesus pays the temple tax, and John 5, when Jesus stirs up controversy by healing a man at the Pool of Bethesda). Nevertheless, although Jesus regularly visits the temple as an observant Jew (at least three times a year), the Gospel record is surprisingly silent regarding His interactions with the Sadducees.

Why is there so little mention of Jesus' interaction with the Sadducees? Perhaps the interactions were insignificant. Perhaps Jesus and the Sadducees mutually ignored each other. Perhaps Jesus' involvement with the Sadducees did not rise to the level of importance in any of the Gospel writers' minds. Or perhaps, Jesus ignored the Sadducees intentionally! Would it strike anyone as odd if an all-star athlete played out his career without ever stopping by the franchise front office? If this happened, it would not be unintentional.

One of the great dangers of success is an inflated ego. How does one lovingly yet effectively attack pride, religious pride at that? Pointing it out is seldom productive; defense mechanisms overpower it. A public put-down can serve to enhance their public stature. Perhaps a better approach, the one taken by Jesus, is to simply ignore them. The most stunning aspect of Jesus' interaction with the Sadducees is how little interaction there is. Powerful people are so accustomed to being shown preferential treatment that it is very hard for them not to expect it. When this happens, the most loving thing one can do is not to give them what they have become accustomed to. Perhaps, like in the mysterious world of dating, love may be demonstrated by purposeful distance designed to draw one in. A measure of aloofness tends to make the attraction all the more—not less—attractive. When we watch Jesus at work among the confident, traditional-minded Sadducees, we notice His benign neglect designed, I suggest, to stimulate the Sadducees' curiosity.

Pragmatism over Principle
(The Pragmatic Sadducees)

Various occupations, including journalists and politicians, are caricatured by the statement, "When they smell blood, there are no principles." The resurrection of Lazarus (John 11:1–44) exposes a very dark side of the Sadducees, their sacrifice of principle for "peace" (John 11:45–57). The popularity of Jesus among the people in and around Jerusalem soars when He raises an already-decaying body to full life. The Sanhedrin convenes to discuss what to do with the undesirable, and now mega-popular, miracle worker. One of the all-time classic statements of pragmatism is found on the lips of the Sadducees' leader, Caiaphas: "You do not realize that it is better for you that one man die for the people than that the whole nation perish" (v. 50). In other words, keeping the peace (and keeping our perks) is more important than standing for justice and truth. Jesus' trial before the Sanhedrin places a huge mirror in front of the Sadducees. Will they compromise principle for pragmatism?

Eventually the Sadducees will witness the death at the cross. Though some will wince in pain as they see a good man suffer, most probably will feel justified, thinking they are protecting the nation at the "nominal price" of one man's life. Certainly they are among those who deeply believe that Jesus' blood is justifiably shed (Matthew 27:25).

Divine Disruption
(The Keepers of the Temple, Round Two)

A marriage counselor was once asked what he would talk about if he had only one hour to converse with a couple about to be married. Without hesitating he responded, "Oh, that's easy. I'd do my best to get them into a fight." Sometimes the most loving thing to do for someone is to provoke a confrontation, to start a fight, to force them off dead center. This Jesus does in His involvement with the Sadducees by cleansing the temple a second time (Matthew 21:12–16; Mark 11:15–18; Luke 19:45–47).

And His provocation works! For the next week the Sadducees are fuming. Unquestionably Jesus is loving—but He is not "nice" or namby-pamby in His dealings with entrenched religious wrongdoing. When we watch Jesus at work among the Sadducees, we notice that He provokes controversy in order to stimulate spiritual self-examination.

Question Authority
(The Credentialing Sadducees)

On Tuesday of the final week of His life, Jesus again enters the temple (Matthew 21:23–27; Mark 11:27–33; Luke 20:1–8), the Sadducees' home turf, and His! Still angry from the previous day's confrontation, the Sadducees demand Jesus' credentials. Unintimidated, Jesus questions theirs. The issue of credentials looms large with people in power. Jesus, the peasant, prophet, priest, and king, possesses the proper credentials for each of these offices. Nevertheless, at every turn He downplays—or more potently dismantles—the superficial credentialing of spiritual leaders. When we watch Jesus at work among the Sadducees, we notice that He insists that divine credentials are infinitely more important than human credentials.

Stinging Tales
(The Storied Sadducees)

While still in the temple, Jesus tells a series of pointed parables that the religious leaders rightly ascertain are about them (Matthew 21:28–22:14; Mark 12:1–12; Luke 20:9–19). Jesus puts the Sadducees into His stories and minces no words in pronouncing God's displeasure of those who profess piety but do not practice it, who are stewards of God's house yet kill God's Son. Stories are often more likely to penetrate human defenses against self-exposure than direct confrontation. Prophet Nathan classically used a story to cut through King David's self-justification (2 Samuel 12). Jesus' thinly-veiled tales are likewise designed to make the Sadducees' choice against Him perfectly unambiguous. When we watch Jesus at work among the Sadducees, we notice that He shoots straight about sin, in a most penetrating fashion, when the stakes are highest.

Saving Ignorance
(The Scholarly Sadducees)

Tuesday's confrontations between Jesus and the Sadducees are not over. As Jesus is agonizingly anticipating the cross, the Sadducees are formulating nonsensical questions (Matthew 22:23–33; Mark 12:18–27; Luke 20:27–40). They address Jesus as "teacher" and pose a "biblical" question about levirate marriage (Deuteronomy 25:5–10) and the resurrection. Their question is akin to the classic, "When did you quit beating your wife?" Vigorously, Jesus turns the loaded question on the questioners with a four-pronged response. First, you are ignorant of the very Scriptures you profess to honor. Second, you refuse to acknowledge the power of the God you say you serve. Third, you not only deny the resurrection, you also distort it. Finally, you have turned the Great "I Am" into an impotent "I Was"!

Few blows are more painful than to be told you are failing in an area of professed and prideful strength. This is precisely what Jesus does. He confronts the best-educated Pentateuch scholars of His day with the charge that they are ignorant of the content and central core of the Scriptures! Scholarship has an often unseen and unacknowledged underside, blinding pride. When we watch Jesus at work among the Sadducees we notice that He has little patience for self-satisfied Scripture-twisting.

Kangaroo Court
(The "Justices")

It is one thing to profess certain ethical principles in the cool of a debate. It is quite another to follow one's stated ethical principles in the heat of battle. The final encounter of Jesus with the Sadducees is a hastily called series of mock trials leading to Jesus' crucifixion. Between Tuesday and Thursday of Holy Week, the Sadducees had plotted to get rid of Jesus.[3] They now feel justified in pushing Him to His execution. The judicial irregularities at Jesus' trial are legion, and this is particularly condemning from a group alleged to be nitpickers when it came to the details of criminal law. The Sadducees' hypocrisy is glaring—but entirely unseen. When we watch Jesus at work among the Sadducees, we notice that He knows which "buttons" to push in order to force them to make a decision about Him—and have to live with it!

WALK WITH JESUS

Though the Sadducees passed off the historical scene almost two thousand years ago, their spirit is still with us today. If you share some of the TENDENCIES of the Sadducees, let me offer some good news and some bad news.

The bad news first. Power is corrupting, and the more we pursue it, the more likely we are to succumb to its pull. Having elite status is addicting, and if we let it go to our heads it will calcify our hearts. Religion is blinding, and if we place too much trust in it we will distance ourselves from God. A penchant for control is controlling. And success affects the psyche, often in spiritually dangerous ways.

If Jesus could spend an afternoon walking and talking with Sadducee-like people today, I suspect He might approach them as He did the Sadducees He met many years ago. Here are questions (a baker's dozen) He might ask:

- How's the fruit growing going? What discrepancies do you see between your religious roots and the spiritual fruit you are producing? How are you dealing with this?
- Religious traditions can easily turn into idols. If I (Jesus) provocatively disrupted one of your most trusted religious institutions or practices, how would you respond? Would you immediately react or take a second look?
- Have the seeming coincidences of your life ever made you wonder about God's active involvement in your life?
- Does it strike you as hypocritical to ignore God and then get ticked when people ignore you? Is it possible that God is trying to pique your interest?
- What passages have you basically cut out of the Scriptures because they don't jibe with your theology, politics, morality, or personal preferences?
- To what extent do you fudge the truth to get what you want? What compromises do you make to maintain

your way of life? Do you sacrifice principle for "peace"?

- What might I (Jesus) do or say to you to get you so mad you'll lose it and be forced to look at your heart?

- Are there people in your life right now whose credentials are lacking but whose wisdom is compelling? And are there people in your life whose credentials are sterling but whose wisdom is suspect? How do you deal with this seeming anomaly?

- Are there any stories you have read or movies you have watched in which you saw yourself in the character of a villain? How did you respond?

- Honestly, how much stock do you place in your intelligence? Do you really think you can figure things out and make things work? What happens when you can't and don't?

- Have you ever become so angry that you lost your head and did or said something really stupid? To what did you attribute your failure? Did it cause you to question your character?

- Have you ever participated in (or indifferently watched play out) the unjust treatment of someone you disliked (or whose views you disliked)?

- In what ways have you been corrupted by the power you possess as a spouse, parent, manager, leader, etc.?

And now for some good news. The Sadducees of old, and today, provide many good, but often overlooked, benefits. Let me cite five.

First, the Sadducees got things done. As power brokers they worked behind the scenes to keep the peace and enhance the prosperity of the subjugated people of Israel.[4] Though the Sadducees may have been disliked by the masses, they did contribute to the reasonably good life the people enjoyed under Roman occupation.

Second, the Sadducees maintained the temple worship. The temple keepers may have been perfunctory in some of what they did. Nevertheless, they followed the rules and rituals given by God to Moses.

A third, and often overlooked, asset of the Sadducees was their refusal to add to the law of God. The Pharisees viewed the oral law and the written law as equal in authority. The Sadducees demurred—as did Jesus!

Fourth, although most religious types scoff at those who eschew the supernatural, there is some unacknowledged value in those who are skeptical of the miraculous. Whereas some see a demon under every bush, a spirit in every success, and a miracle in every blessing, more skeptical types attribute such to natural forces, and often they may be correct.

A final blessing of the much-maligned Sadducees was their maintenance of the traditions. Those who protect the "old ways" are seldom popular. Nevertheless, it is easy to overlook the repository of wisdom the traditions embody. The Sadducees sought to preserve the ancient words and ways of God.

And there is one small piece of very good news about the Sadducees mentioned by Dr. Luke in Acts 6:7. "A large number of priests became obedient to the faith." By all accounts, some of these priests must have been Sadducees. What happened? Perhaps they were sickened by the judicial irregularities and heinous behavior of their leaders. Or they may have softened as they watched a good man die with unique dignity. The tearing of the temple curtain and the timing of the earthquake may have caught their attention (Matthew 27:51). Eyewitness news of the resurrection of Jesus may have jolted their philosophical prejudices (Matthew 28). The way the early church handled the widow crisis may have caught their eye (Acts 6:1-6). Certainly it was the power of the Holy Spirit!

Whatever the precipitating factors, God's family includes former power brokers who found themselves broken at the foot of the cross!

WORK FOR JESUS

How might you be more useful and effective in representing Jesus to people you meet who are leaders or in places of power and influence, who are Sadducee-like in background and outlook? Here are seven areas to consider as you interact with these traditionalists.

1. Making a Connection

Making a connection with a "Sadducee" may be difficult for two reasons: Sadducee-like people are few in number and they may well be outside one's natural circle of acquaintance. But they are precious to God. Jesus connected with the Sadducees on their turf, the temple, and on their terms, the mind. Modern-day "Sadducees" are more likely to occupy offices than temple edifices. But their modus operandi is still highly rational. They seek, more than any of the other spiritual profiles, to synthesize Scripture with science and the mystical with the intellectual, normally giving preference to the latter over the former. They want their religion, and their secular worldview too. You may be interacting with such Sadducees daily.

Jesus connected with the Sadducees by provoking thought. He piqued their curiosity, threw them intellectual curve balls, pointed out their contradictions, even questioned their intelligence, and goaded them to think deeply about spiritual matters.

Some years ago I taught a class on the life of Jesus. After the third session a woman approached me and made one of the strangest comments I had ever heard. She said,

"Tom, you don't appear to be a moron." Of course I was shocked by her statement, so I asked her what she meant. She replied, "You and the people in this class appear to be reasonably intelligent, and you believe the Bible to be true. I have been taught since childhood [in a very liberal Christian denomination] that those who believe the Bible have deficient IQs." It is hard to believe one could live well into adulthood believing such an outrageous lie. Nevertheless, those who are well educated, well connected, and well endowed financially may not get outside their circles very often. This woman, for one, was shocked and impressed with "reasonably intelligent" people who could articulate their faith in God's Word.

2. The Tone of the Conversation

Of all of the spiritual profiles with whom He interacted, Jesus was most direct with the Sadducees. He minced no words. Generally, those who "tell it like it is" do so partly because they feel secure (and powerful) enough not to worry overmuch what people think of them. Moreover, they carry an air of importance with regard to the use of time. Thus, they shoot straight and respect those who do likewise. However, the tendency of most people in the presence of the "rich and powerful" is to kowtow to them or seek to schmooze them. Jesus was neither so insecure that He needed their approval, nor overly impressed with pomp and power.

Nor should we! Actually we can better represent Jesus if we, like He, do not show favoritism toward people.

A Navy officer of my acquaintance told me that a common adage in his profession states, "Once you become a captain, no one is going to tell you the truth, they are going to tell you their agenda." A great danger of power is being distanced from the truth—particularly about oneself. Followers of Jesus do a great service to Sadducean-like people when we appropriately speak the truth in love.

3. Finding Common Ground

The common ground Jesus shared with the Sadducees was, ironically, their authority. The Sadducees were bred to be in control. They saw themselves as the authoritative interpreters of the law, the authorized keepers of God's temple, and the wardens to watch for any unauthorized claimants of religious authority. I suspect they were the most likely of the spiritual profiles to feel secure in who they were and what they were supposed to do. Not surprisingly, their major problem with Jesus was His "lack" of authority.

Jesus could have mounted a campaign to defend His authority. But He didn't. Instead, He simply lived out His higher sense of authority derived from oneness with His Father.

In the eighteenth century, the British Parliament voted

to offer a huge financial reward to anyone who could produce an accurate instrument to measure longitude at sea. Some of the greatest scientists who have ever lived worked on the project unsuccessfully. Finally, John Harrison, a Yorkshire carpenter and clockmaker, produced a successful marine chronometer. It took him years, however, to receive his due reward, in part due to his lack of credentials. Representatives of Jesus must find their security, authority, and credentials primarily in Him as they lovingly build common ground with the powerful.

4. Losing the Found

The Sadducees certainly considered themselves among the "found." They were God's chosen people, part of God's covenant family, keepers of the law and the temple, and the ones who made the sacrifices happen. They did not know the extent to which they were lost. Likewise, in our world today, there are people who are deeply religious; they are grateful participants in the rituals of religion who have little sense of being lost. How did Jesus seek to get the "found" Sadducees lost? Primarily, He provoked them in ways that made their deep-seated prejudices and well-hidden injustices come pouring out.

Representing Jesus, how can we be used as godly goads with the goal of bringing people to the Gospel? Jesus did it by pointing to sources the Sadducees acknowledged as authoritative, on turf they claimed as their own, and calling into question items they most prided themselves on: education, legislation, power, and religion. Representing Jesus with Sadducee-like spiritual profiles will require a keen eye for inconsistencies and a wise approach to their exposure.

5. Surprisingly . . .

Two things about Jesus' interactions with the Sadducees surprise and instruct me. First, Jesus typically avoided the Sadducees. The Sadducees were at the epicenter of Judaism. To have recruited the Sadducees into His camp would have been a real spiritual coup—or would it? I would have tried much harder to reach them and probably overreached. Jesus knew better.

Power plays in religious settings are very common. Having been bitten, I have become a bit wiser. At first when I was "wined and dined" or "dressed down" by power brokers, I either found myself flattered and then flattened, or I cowered and capitulated. I learned, however, that when I smell power plays, the best (and most loving) approach is to "play dumb" and say little. To play power games with the powerful is to play into their hand—and sacrifice their souls. In my experience "benign neglect" either humbles power players or infuriates them. Both hopefully will lead them to the cross.

Second, I am surprised by Jesus' cultural clash with the Sadducees. We tend to believe that we are best suited to reach "our kind of people." However, when Jesus interacted with the Sadducees two subcultures clashed. Jesus was a Galilean peasant; the Sadducees were Judean aristocrats. Jesus had only an average education at best; the Sadducees were well educated. Jesus was poor; the Sadducees were rich. Nevertheless, Jesus stirred the souls of the Sadducees like none other.

There is a surprising pattern in Scripture, and sometimes in real life, of elites being instructed by "fools." One of the obvious disadvantages of being powerful is that you don't know who to trust. So you become suspicious of everyone except a "fool." It is not by accident that frequently God uses humble servants (often literally servants) to get through to the hearts of the powerful. God used a slave girl to capture the heart of a Syrian general (2 Kings 5). God used a simple shepherd, Amos, to confront the rich and powerful in the Middle East. God used a kidnapped boy, Daniel, to speak truth to Nebuchadnezzar, the most powerful man in the world. God used the power of peasants who had been with Jesus to get through to the hearts of the "priests."

In more recent times, God used a housekeeper, Maria Millis, to show the love of God to the lonely Anthony Ashley Cooper, later Lord Shaftsbury, champion of the poor. God also used a Lilliputian giant named Mother Teresa to speak truth to presidents and prime ministers. And God is using poor African church leaders to confound the rich and powerful—and wayward—West. To reach out to power people we must, like Jesus, be worthy of trust, people of integrity. "Fools" can often cut through to power people partly because they are too "dumb" to understand power, but smart enough to know God!

6. Slogans and Symbols

The slogan of Hebrew National hot dogs is, "We Answer to a Higher Authority." The Sadducees seemed to lose sight of the Higher Authority they ostensibly served. Those who are on the top of the pyramid are positioned and programmed to look down rather than up. Jesus, through provocative acts, penetrating words, a painful death, and a puzzling resurrection, sought to lift the Sadducees' eyes to see a much higher authority—and to question their man-centered approach to life.

I was so startled one afternoon on a busy avenue in Denver that I nearly crashed my car. We passed by a church sign that read in big letters: "Progressive Values in a Traditional Setting." Immediately I blurted out to two of my children who were with me, "That is the diametric opposite of everything Jesus stood for." I suspect that those who came up with the words on the sign were trying to proclaim to passersby that this church was both "culturally cool" and "traditionally sensitive." They boldly advertised their willingness to assert their cultural authority while denying God's. Sad indeed!

7. Connecting with Jesus

The ultimate question Jesus wanted every spiritual profile to wrestle with was His identity and the implications thereof. And the way Jesus presented Himself to each spiritual profile was uniquely fitting. With the Sadducees Jesus connected Himself inextricably with the temple. At age twelve, Jesus, just after a discussion with teachers in the temple, called the place of worship "my Father's house" (Luke 2:49). At the outset of His public ministry Jesus, after having cleansed the temple, said, "Destroy this temple, and I will raise it again in three days" (John 2:19). In his mock trial before the Sanhedrin (mainly Sadducees), false witnesses were solicited to accuse Jesus of threatening, like a terrorist, to destroy the temple (Matthew 26:61; Mark 14:58). And the moment Jesus died, "the curtain of the temple was torn in two from top to bottom" (Matthew 27:51). Then three days later Jesus fulfilled His words about the "sign of Jonah" (Matthew 16:4) and the three-day rebuilding of His temple.

Jesus earnestly longed for the Sadducees to see that He fulfilled all of the promises and practices of the temple, and that their temple would soon be destroyed. He longed for them to see that God had "tabernacled" among them (John 1:14) and now wanted to tabernacle within them (1 Corinthians 6:19; Colossians 1:27).

J. R. R. Tolkien's trilogy, The Lord of the Rings, graphically portrays the corrupting power of power. The most powerful good characters in the story—Gandalf, Elrond, and Galadriel—refuse to take the ring, which will equally empower and enslave them. Recognition of this reality should give us a large measure of compassion for the powerful as we seek to free them.

An Introduction

Wherever there are two Jews you will have three opinions, the first Jew's opinion, the second Jew's opinion and G-d's opinion.

5

LET'S MEET *the* PHARISEES

We have more data about the Pharisees than any of the other spiritual profiles by far. They are mentioned by name almost one hundred times in the New Testament and referred to scores more. They are the chief architects of rabbinic Judaism, whose views are reflected in the Mishnah (oral law) and the Talmud, and whose influence is dominant to today. And they represent the spiritual profiles with whom Jesus interacted the most—the do gooders and truth seekers.

The Pharisees dominated the religious landscape of Israel in Jesus' day. Though they were not the keepers of the temple (the Sadducees were), nor numerous (Josephus states their number to be six thousand), nor politically well connected, they dominated the synagogues that were scattered throughout the land and thereby controlled the dominant religious ideas of the time in Israel. They represented the mainstream Jews who took their spirituality seriously and sought to live by God's commandments. Today they would be called by names such as orthodox, moderate, conservative, fundamental, and so on. Moreover, by all accounts, the Pharisees seem to include the spiritual profiles that most resembled Jesus and the disciples.

INTRODUCING THE PHARISEES

The Pharisees, no doubt, would trace their roots back to God. To do otherwise would be unthinkable. God established a covenantal relationship with Abraham, the father of the Jewish people, and the father of faith. But it was Moses, the great lawgiver, who gave the Jewish people their greatest legacy, God's righteous commandments—613 of them to understand and obey. This, the Pharisees believed, was both a great privilege and a great responsibility.

It was Moses, according to the rabbis in Jesus' day, who gave to the Jewish people two laws. The written law was enshrined in what we today call the Pentateuch or the first five books of the Old Testament. The oral law (Mishnah), also given by God according to the Jewish rabbis, was to be passed on from generation to generation and reflect the application of God's timeless law to changing times. The Mishnah stated God's command thusly: "Moses received the Law from Sinai and committed it to Joshua, and Joshua to the elders, and the elders to the Prophets; and the Prophets committed it to the men of the Great Synagogue. They said three things: Be deliberate in judgment, raise up many disciples, and make a fence around the Law."[1]

The law of God was supposed to be the constitution by which Israel ruled the nation, the life of the community, the family, and the individual. Israel was supposed to be a people set apart to and for God. This holiness was to be reflected in Israel's religious life, centered in God's glorious temple in Jerusalem. Israel's history, however, tells the sad story of Jewish "idolatry, immorality, and bloodshed," three reasons the rabbis cited for Jerusalem's destruction in 586 BC.

The people of Israel were taken into exile to Babylon. Now, separated from the temple and its rituals and sacrifices, a fresh emphasis on the study of the law emerged. Ezra, the scribe, became a prototype of a new kind of spiritual leader. Ezra 7:10 records, "For Ezra had devoted himself to the study and observance of the Law of the Lord, and to teaching its decrees and laws in Israel."

The people of Israel were eventually allowed to return to their ancestral homeland, rebuild their temple, and resume their traditional religious practices. However, now they found themselves under the thumb of occupying nations. And, as can be expected, these occupying powers had a major impact on the mind-set of the people. It was during the period after Jerusalem's destruction and before the time of Jesus, known as the intertestamental period (ca. 433–5 BC), that the Pharisees emerged as an identifiable group.

It was primarily the influence of Alexander the Great (356–323 BC), and the Greek culture that he sought to spread around the world, that gave rise to the Pharisees. As noted in chapter 4, rising opposition to Hellenism (embodied in the Seleucids in Syria) climaxed in the Maccabean Revolt that would ultimately overthrow the Syrians and establish an independent Jewish state for about one hundred years (166–63 BC).

The first historical mention of the Pharisees is in the writings of Josephus regarding the reign of Jonathan Maccabaeus (161–142 BC).[2] But the first historical event in which the Pharisees are involved takes place during the reign of John Hyrcanus I (134–104 BC). Here we find the Pharisees as a group at odds with the king over the issue of the priesthood, for Hyrcanus was both king and high priest. This caused the king to side with the sympathetic Sadducees and oppose the Pharisees. This opposition to the Pharisees turned violent under the reign of Hyrcanus's son,

Alexander Jannaeus (103–76 BC). The Pharisees, however, operating through the synagogues scattered throughout the country, had the hearts of the people with them. Jannaeus, on his deathbed, advised his wife and successor, Salome Alexandra (76–67 BC), to work with the Pharisees because they held great power with the people.[3] The queen took her husband's advice, and the Pharisees attained a large measure of political power during her reign, and sometimes abused that power. After her death, the Pharisees never again attained the measure of political clout they had under the queen.

In 63 BC the Romans swept into Israel, ending the decrepit Hasmonean Dynasty. The Jews again lost their independence. During the siege of Jerusalem led by Herod, some Pharisees apparently advised surrender. This resulted in a favorable relationship between the Pharisees and the government during the reign of Herod the Great (37–4 BC). But after the death of Herod, which coincides with the birth of Jesus, the Pharisees always seemed to play second fiddle to other groups politically, even though they continued to dominate the religious life of the Jewish people.

HILLEL AND SHAMMAI

Two of the greatest Jewish rabbis who ever lived spearheaded the religious life of Israel at the changing of BC to

AD. Hillel and Shammai were both alive when Jesus was born (ca. 4 BC). Much of the oral tradition of the first century that is recorded in the Mishnah is derived from the teachings of Hillel and Shammai and their respective followers (or "schools"). Although actual recorded statements of Hillel and Shammai are few, the disagreements between their schools are numerous. And although there is strong agreement between these two great rabbis about the big picture of Jewish theology, they disagree mightily over the details. On numerous points of the Mosaic law the two schools take differing opinions.

Even the casual reader of the New Testament encounters the ubiquitous Pharisees. They are present on almost every page of the Gospels. When Christians read about the Pharisees, (often referred to in the Gospels as "the Jews"), we normally think of a monolithic group of hypocritical Christ-haters. This view is seriously erroneous on two counts. First, the Pharisees were not a monolithic group. Many important distinctions existed among the various Pharisee factions. Second, the Pharisees were not all Christ-haters. The truth is that most of the Pharisees were very good people. But they had spiritual flaws that Jesus clearly saw and exposed, because He loved them dearly, as we will see in chapters 6 and 7.

Though we present two different spiritual profiles arising from the two great Pharisaic leaders, remember, that their core beliefs were similar. The similarities and differences between them are analogous to the similarities and differences between evangelicals and fundamentalists, who would readily sign each other's doctrinal statements but disagree heartily over the interpretation and application of the details of the Scriptures. Once I have identified the salient traits of the two Pharisee spiritual profiles, I will then apply these traits to the Gospel texts and seek to identify which kind of Pharisee Jesus is interacting with, and what that means for us.

DIFFERENCES BETWEEN HILLEL AND SHAMMAI

Let me briefly suggest ten differences between Hillel and Shammai:

1. Hillel had a heart for the poor and Shammai had a mind for precision. Hillel, born in Babylonia, moved penniless to Palestine. He supported himself as a woodcutter as he devoted himself to the study of the Torah. Shammai was from Palestine and worked as an engineer or surveyor. Not surprisingly, Hillel wanted to reach out to people and Shammai wanted to be right.

2. Hillel was patient even with the impertinent, whereas Shammai didn't "suffer fools gladly." A famous story

is told of a Gentile who came to Shammai and sought to become a convert to Judaism if Shammai could summarize the Torah while standing on one leg. Shammai was angry at the audacious request and chased the Gentile away with a stick. The Gentile then came to Hillel and offered the same conditions. Hillel, apparently while standing on one leg, answered, "What is hateful to you, do not do to your fellow: this is the whole Law; the rest is the explanation; go and learn."[4]

3. Shammai was professorial and Hillel was pastoral. Both Hillel and Shammai loved, studied, practiced, and taught the Holy Scriptures. However, Hillel's method of teaching was more relational and Socratic, whereas Shammai's method was more intellectual and didactic.

4. Shammai saw God's commands as absolute and rigid while Hillel was more flexible and accommodating. Hillel joyously lived in booths during the Feast of Tabernacles, but allowed for reasonable exceptions. Not so, decreed Shammai. So intent was he on strictly keeping the Feast that when his daughter-in-law gave birth during Tabernacles, Shammai removed part of the roof of the house overhanging the bed in which the baby lay and placed green branches so as to provide a proper booth.[5]

5. Hillel generally emphasized the logic of the law and Shammai the letter of the law. The Day of Atonement was the only required fast among the Jews. Was anyone excluded from this command? Hillel said that children shouldn't be required to fast while Shammai said they should. Should a bride be told that she is beautiful on her wedding day even if she is not? Shammai said that the truth should always be told. Hillel said that a bride was always beautiful on her wedding day. Is one's posture important when one recites the Shema (Deuteronomy 6:4–7)? Shammai said, "Yes, because it says so." Hillel said the intent of the heart is what matters.[6] Shammai insisted on the literal meaning of God's law whereas Hillel was more inclined to accept a literary meaning.

6. Hillel was liberal with permissions whereas Shammai was conservative. Thus Hillel allowed a man to divorce his wife for almost any cause whereas Shammai forbade it except in cases of marital unfaithfulness.[7]

7. Shammai's default mode generally was no and Hillel's was yes. Thus in most of the rulings in the Mishnah, Hillel and his school are lenient and Shammai and his followers were hard line. For example, one of Hillel's most important rulings dealt with figuring out a way for both debtor and creditor to be satisfied financially on the Sabbatical Year.[8]

8. Shammai required his students to demonstrate their commitment before enrolling in his classes whereas Hillel was more inclined to invite his students to come before they had proven their commitment.

9. Shammai was more inclined to separate himself from Gentiles and nonobservant Jews, and Hillel was less. Hillel sought to maintain good relations with all people, including Gentiles. Shammai, as reflected in his Eighteen Edicts, insisted on strict separation between Jews and non-Jews.

10. Hillel and Shammai leaned different directions on the political continuum, Hillel leaning more toward the Romans and Shammai leaned away. The Hillelites favored conciliation for the sake of peace, and the Shammaites favored confrontation for the sake of freedom.

In the following two chapters we will apply many of these differences to the New Testament accounts that simply say "the Pharisees" or "the Jews" without specifying which kind. By specifying which kind of Pharisee Jesus is dealing with, we will learn how He dealt with two very significant, yet different, spiritual profiles differently—and how we can help those who fit the profiles of the do gooders and truth seekers as well.

Profile:
The Hillel Pharisees

A religious man is a person who holds God and man in one thought at one time, at all times, who suffers harm done to others, whose greatest passion is compassion, whose greatest strength is love and defiance of despair.

—ABRAHAM JOSHUA HESCHEL

JESUS *and the* DO GOODERS

Why do those who behave badly always make the headlines, and those who do good seldom seem to get any press? If what we read and see in the media was all we knew about religious people, we would have to conclude that they are a bunch of self-righteous, racist, greedy, ignorant, child-molesting, hate-mongering hypocrites. We all know that there are a few who do fit the just-mentioned categories. However, anyone with an ounce of fairness would have to admit that the majority of religious folk are good, decent people. And a sizable number are "salt of the earth" kind of people.

As a local church pastor for almost thirty years, I have

encountered all kinds of people in the churches I have pastored. And yes, some have been bad and done ugly things. But most of the people I know are genuinely good (I use "good" in a relative, not an absolute sense). They play by the rules and pay their taxes, get along well with others and make good neighbors, are sincerely compassionate, do good deeds for good reasons, are modest and humble, work and play hard, and faithfully execute their duties with a cheerful attitude. They are good with their money, are upstanding citizens, use their words well, are faithful to their marriage vows and to their family, and are fun-loving but do not live to party. And add to this the fact that they earnestly seek to know and obey God, though sometimes they do neither. I submit that the number of such people in any religious group is not small, even if it is regularly overlooked.

Sometimes such people are called Goody Two-shoes, or other unkind titles. Sometimes they are ridiculed as being stuck-in-the-mud or boring. Sometimes they are viewed with suspicion as if they are hiding some diabolical faults. Sometimes they are considered too-good-to-be-true. But you can't deny the fact that in most of our spheres of relationship there are people who are truly good. Seldom does this group of people receive their due.

INTRODUCING
HILLEL THE ELDER

If ever the "do gooders" had a hero, it was Hillel the Elder, who was born about 60 BC into a Jewish family in Babylon and died about AD 10 or 20. Nothing is known of his childhood and little of his time in Babylon. He had a brother, Shebna, who was a merchant, while Hillel was a woodcutter and Torah teacher. Also according to legend, Hillel's life paralleled that of Moses.

At some point in his life, while Caesar Augustus ruled in Rome and Herod the Great ruled in Israel, Hillel moved to Jerusalem to take up the study of the law. He was so poor that he could not afford the tuition fee. However, he was determined to study under two of the great Scripture scholars, Shemaiah and Abtalion. The story goes that Hillel climbed up on the snowy roof of the rabbinical school and peered through a skylight so as to learn from the learned rabbis. He was found frozen half to death on the roof and the sincerity of his desire to study the Jewish Scriptures so moved the teachers that they changed the policy of having to pay for rabbinical education.

When the pair of teachers, Shemaiah and Abtalion, passed on, they were replaced by another pair of eminent teachers, Hillel and Shammai. Hillel's ascendancy to leadership (also according to legend) was occasioned by his wisdom in settling a question about sacrificial rituals. While in leadership of the Sanhedrin, Hillel is credited with creating principles of Scripture interpretation ("Seven Rules of Hillel") and the structure ("Orders") of the Mishnah.

Hillel is most famous in Judaism for his formulation of the Golden Rule. He was approached by a Gentile (who had been summarily dismissed by Shammai) desiring to become a Jewish proselyte if Hillel could teach him the essence of Judaism while standing on one foot. Hillel replied, "What is hateful to you, do not to your neighbor: that is the whole Torah, while the rest is commentary thereof; go and learn it"[1] His negative formulation of the Golden Rule preceded Jesus' by a few decades. In his answer, Hillel acknowledged the centrality of love as the essence of the Hebrew religion (cf. Leviticus 19:18).

By all accounts, Hillel loved the Scriptures and sought to make them understandable and applicable to life in the real world. To this day Hillel is considered to be one of the greatest rabbis who ever lived, a forerunner of rabbinic Judaism; and Jewish centers all over the world bear his name.

TENDENCIES of the "Hillel Pharisees"

Truth: Hillel and his followers regarded the Mosaic Law (the written law) as the primary source of truth as supplemented by the wise interpretations of learned rabbis (the oral law, or Mishnah). God's truth is derived from skillful exegesis of Scripture and wise application to real-life situations. All of life comes under the supervision of God's truth and traditions.

E*conomics:* Hillel was a man of modest means, and his followers were mostly working class farmers and shopkeepers. They had regular incomes and sufficient leisure that they could devote some time to study.

N*eighborhood:* Even though many scholars believe the name "Pharisee" is derived from a word meaning "separated ones," they were not as separate as you might imagine. Participation in the community was a high value to Hillel and his followers. Hillel encouraged the cultivation of habits like loyalty, humility, and compassion that make one an excellent contributing member of a community. Josephus saw them as being "affectionate to each other," and he said that they cultivated "harmonious relations with the community unlike the Sadducees."[2]

D*evotion:* Hillel's approach to living the spiritual life involved first being a part of God's covenant family, then repenting of sin, receiving God's forgiveness, making restitution where appropriate, and living a life of loyalty to God's law.

E*veryman:* Hillel looked on human beings as valuable (made in the image of God and elected by grace) and volitional (given freedom to choose to obey God). Thus, they have a duty to care for themselves and others. Too much trust in oneself, however, is unwise.

N*ature of God:* E. P. Sanders summarizes the Pharisees' theology: "The Pharisees believed that God was good, that he created the world, that he governed it, and that it would turn out as he wished.... God is perfectly reliable and will keep all his promises.... He can be relied on to punish disobedience and reward obedience. He is just; therefore he never does the reverse. When it comes to punishment, however, his justice is moderated by mercy and by his promises."[3] The love, mercy, and forgiveness of God would have particularly resonated among Hillel and his followers.

C*ivics:* Hillel and his followers were political moderates, slightly to the right of center. Though they were not fond of Roman rule, they realized that opposition to it was futile. They appreciated the peace and freedom to worship that Roman government offered. Thus, they saw themselves as part of the opposition advocating principled submission to Rome.

I*mmortality:* Though vague with specifics, the Pharisees believed in an afterlife. Since God is just, He will punish sin and reward obedience. Some form of eternal punishment awaits the few very evil, annihilation results for those outside or disobedient to the covenant, and eternal reward awaits the righteous.

E*thics:* Hillel can rightly be credited with promoting Golden Rule ethics since he formulated a version of the Rule before Jesus. Ethics must be based on law and love.

S*ummary:* The law of devotion to God and love of man stood at the heart of Hillel's approach to life.

WATCH JESUS

How did Jesus interact with the followers of Hillel in His day? Consider these eight encounters.

Nic at Night
(Nicodemus)

Nicodemus is the first recorded Pharisee with whom Jesus interacts (John 3:1–21). He is a leading Pharisee who seems to have the spirit of Hillel. Nicodemus seeks out Jesus, greets Him respectfully, acknowledges His miracles and draws a correct theological conclusion, and seems sincerely interested in Jesus' perspective. I suspect Rabbi Nicodemus wants to have a cordial evening theological conversation. Jesus, however, responds to Nicodemus with a zinger completely out of left field. Using the concept of birth, Jesus tells Nicodemus he needs a radical transformation. In essence Jesus says, "To even be able to see the kingdom of God, one must be born again." Nicodemus doesn't get it. So to make things more difficult, Jesus affirms that not only must one be born again, but this birth must be from above. Nicodemus doesn't get this either. So to make things even more difficult, Jesus affirms that this birth will arise out of death. Nicodemus' reaction to this is not noted, but he must have wondered if he had met a "man from Mars."

Nicodemus reappears at Jesus' death, accompanied by Joseph of Arimathea, another Pharisee of the Hillelite persuasion. Together they receive permission from the authorities to take Jesus' body, prepare it for burial, and place it in a garden tomb (John 19:38–42; cf. Luke 23: 50–53). Perhaps these two Pharisees have become believers in the Jesus as Messiah.

When we watch Jesus at work with a good-hearted follower of Hillel, we notice that He immediately introduces a radical theological paradigm. Nicodemus is probably interested in being a better rabbi; Jesus wants him to see that he needs to become a better baby. And watching the final actions of Nicodemus and Joseph, we are reminded that some Pharisees are very good—and some are even courageous, willing to come out from among their peers and the politicians. Jesus knows that only a radical reorientation of heart characterized by childlike dependence and trust will result in eternal life.

"Which of Them Will Love Him More?" (Simon the Pharisee)

A common Christian impression of the biblical Pharisees is that they all were a bunch of hypocritical scoundrels. This picture is untrue. Most Pharisees were good and God-fearing. In Luke 7:36–50 we read of a Pharisee named Simon who invited Jesus to dinner.[4] While it is possible that Simon had ill intent, perhaps trying to trap Jesus, it is also possible that he simply wanted to engage Jesus in conversation to learn. Because of the dinner invitation, I suspect that the Pharisee was a follower of Hillel.

Whatever Simon's intentions, everything changed when a woman with a past entered and began washing Jesus' feet with perfume and tears. Her heart obviously had been moved by Jesus' message, and she wanted to return the favor in a tangible way. Jesus was touched, but Simon was troubled. He thought, "A real prophet would have rebuked the woman and told her to straighten up her act and stop this scandalous show." Jesus responded to Simon's thoughts with a short story, a stinging rebuke, a moral, and an offer. When we watch Jesus at work with basically good people we notice that He acknowledges one of the deficits of goodness is a deficient sense of sin—and consequently an inadequate appreciation of forgiveness.

"My Daughter Is Dying"
(Jairus)

Most of the Pharisees who initiated contact with Jesus were likely to have been followers of Hillel rather than separatistic Shammai. Also Hillel's people would likely have had a more tolerant and humble attitude toward alternative truths. So when a synagogue official faces the death of his only daughter, he prostrates himself before the miracle-working rabbi (Matthew 9:18–26; Mark 5:22–43; Luke 8:41–56). Jesus sees a broken and frightened man with a fledgling faith. And Jesus responds to his request with a too-good-to-be-true miracle. Surprisingly Jesus then instructs the elated parents to keep what they had seen in confidence. When we watch Jesus at work among the Pharisees, we notice that He blesses the broken.

"He Wanted to Justify Himself"
(The Justifying Pharisee)

One of the deepest urges of the human heart is to justify ourselves. Children "learn" to blame-shift almost as soon as they can talk. As they mature, the blame game only becomes more sophisticated (and sometimes more comical). In Luke 10:25–37 an "expert in the law" who has an advanced case of "self-justification-itis" meets the Great Physician, Jesus. I think the law expert is a follower of

Hillel because he comes to Jesus, quotes Hillel, and attests that he lives a good life.

Jesus responds to the law scholar with a simple story, the parable of the good Samaritan. In this story Jesus, like a surgeon of the soul, wields three sharp scalpels. First, He cuts into the man's exaggerated sense of personal goodness by showing him to be just like the indifferent priest and Levite. Second, He cuts into the man's superficial sense of God's goodness by showing, in the Samaritan, the lofty requirements of true righteousness. And third, He cuts into the man's egotistical sense of superiority by making a scum-of-the-earth Samaritan the hero of the story. When we watch Jesus at work with good Pharisees, we notice that He cuts deep into the sinews of self-righteousness.

Dinner Conversation
(The Prominent Pharisee)

A Pharisee of high standing invites Jesus over for Sabbath dinner, and the conversation that follows is provocative (Luke 14:1–24). The meal seems to be a setup designed to get Jesus to slip up. I suppose this was akin to the media at a political fund-raising dinner watching for a candidate to put his foot in his mouth. Rather than play it safe, however, Jesus goes on the offensive and questions the questioners, admonishes the editorialists, and tells a story to the gossip columnists. First, Jesus heals a disabled man and questions the Pharisees about the lawfulness of His actions. They become silent, but Jesus rubs it in by pointing out the inconsistencies of their position. Next, Jesus notices the jockeying for position that characterized the invited guests. With both barrels blazing, Jesus admonishes the guests that seat assignments are not true indicators of worth on earth or in heaven. Finally, Jesus contrasts their dinner to the banquet in heaven. When we watch Jesus at work among the Pharisees we notice that He is constantly goading them to examine their boxes, their hearts, and their excuses.

Slave Driver!
(The Elder Brother)

Luke 15 is a landmark text on the Pharisees. Their well-hidden spiritual flaws are laid bare by the all-seeing eye of Jesus. The chapter begins once again with Jesus eating. Apparently Jesus is an A-list invitee. Complaints from the Pharisees about the "sinners" with whom Jesus hung out prompt Jesus' telling of the parable of the prodigal son.

While the departure, repentance, and return of the "prodigal" are heart warming, it is the recalcitrance of the elder brother that is most instructive for the Hillel spiritual profile. The elder brother is on one level a model of goodness. He keeps his inheritance in the homestead while his brother absconds with his. He is responsible while his brother is irresponsible. He obeys the household rules while his brother breaks them. He "pleases" his father's heart while his brother breaks his father's heart.

However, unseen spiritual viruses are reproducing in the elder brother's body. His nose-to-the-grindstone approach to life has degenerated into seeing his father as a slave driver. His demand for fairness has blinded him to grace. His brother's overtly bad behavior has made him oblivious to his own bad attitudes. And his father's kindness has fueled cosmic hatred for both his brother and his father.

The parable of the prodigal son has no nice ending. Jesus doesn't conclude with the words, "And they all lived happily ever after," because they don't! The elder brother continues to stew in his works-righteous juices. When we watch Jesus at work among the good we notice that He knows the fatal flaws of the "righteous" heart; and His grace often brings it out.

"What Good Thing Must I Do to Get Eternal Life?" (The Rich Young Ruler)

The man we call the "rich young ruler" was a good man (Matthew 19:16–30; Mark 10:17–31; Luke 18:18–30). He engages Jesus rather than shuns Him. He "fell on his knees" (Mark 10:17), a sign of humility. He addresses Jesus politely and seems to ask a sincere question about salvation. In fact, the young man asks three good questions in search of answers. When Jesus points to keeping the commandments, the man honestly affirms that he strived to do so. And when Jesus heightened the expectations of God, the man became sad rather than mad. The man's attitude and demeanor parallel that of Hillel.

So how does Jesus interact with a good, orthodox, sincere, humble, young man in search of God? Jesus challenges his assumptions, intensifies his introspection, and raises the standards of God.

The young man's words betray a belief that people can be good (presumably by their efforts to follow God's law). Jesus immediately challenges this conclusion, declaring that only God is good. In a sly way, Jesus is also asking the young man to connect the dots regarding His identity. Then Jesus asks the young man, who has already been told by Jesus that no one is good enough to inherit eternal life, to look at his life in light of the Ten Commandments. In a response that I consider to be sincere, the young man expresses his commitment to obey God. I suspect that he deeply believes that fidelity to the Law is what pleases God.

Then Jesus throws a knuckle ball, the likes of which the man has not seen before: "Give everything you have to the poor and follow Me." This seems extreme! But it is necessitated by the man's goodness.

The greatest danger of the followers of Hillel, ancient and modern, is ironically their goodness. Those who study the Scriptures and seek to follow them in the real world among real people, who understand the basic thrust of the Law to be love of God and man, and who pursue God with humility generally stick out for their goodness in society. Yet a monumental spiritual chasm exists between striving to be righteous before God and receiving the righteousness of God, between pursuing God and acknowledging His pursuit of us. Jesus sought to break a "good man" in order to make him a godly man.

"Which Is the Greatest Commandment?" (The Testing Pharisee)

Perhaps it was a follower of Hillel who asked Jesus, within hours of His crucifixion, a question Jesus had answered before and on which beloved Hillel had spoken clearly, "Which is the greatest commandment in the Law?" (Matthew 22:34–40; Mark 12:28–31).

Jesus sees no problem at all with the recognized answer to this catechetical question. Like the rabbis before Him, Jesus quotes Deuteronomy 6:5 and Leviticus 19:18. Maybe Jesus knows the defenses of the Pharisees too well to bother zeroing in, at this time, on the disconnection between their correct summarization and the incorrect application. A more fundamental issue is at stake, namely "Who is Jesus?" It's a question we also must ask those do gooders who try to please God only by keeping the law.

So Jesus, usually the questioned, becomes the questioner

(Matthew 22:41–46; Mark 12:35–37; Luke 20:41–44). How, Jesus asked the Pharisees, can the Messiah be both the son of David (Isaiah 11:1–2; Jeremiah 23:5–6; Ezekiel 34:23–24) and David's Lord (Psalm 110:1)? Apparently, both Jesus and the Pharisees have said enough, from this point forward, no words will be exchanged. There comes a time when words fail and only actions count. That time has been reached.

WALK WITH JESUS

Perhaps the best way to highlight the commendable aspects and point out the dangers of Hillelian Pharisaism is to compare and contrast Hillel and Jesus.

It is not surprising that many have undertaken to compare Hillel and his younger contemporary, Jesus of Nazareth.[5] Both were working class individuals; Hillel was a woodcutter and Jesus a carpenter. Thus, they had a natural understanding of and appeal to the average man on the streets of Israel. Both were learned in and loved the Holy Scriptures. Thus, they agreed that the basic thrust of the entire Law was the love of God and the love of neighbor. Hillel and Jesus agreed that the Golden Rule captured the essence of how to treat others. Thus, both maintained many wholesome relationships. Both took the business of disciple-making very seriously, devoting most of their time and talent to passing on their teaching to the next generation. Thus, both left lasting legacies. Though both primarily ministered to their own people, they were kind to outsiders and Gentiles. And both were known by their followers for their goodness.

Nevertheless, there were significant differences between Hillel and Jesus. Although Hillel and Jesus were lovers of Scripture, they differed markedly regarding the authority of the oral law. Hillel was a firm believer in its authority and contributed significantly to its substance. Jesus was an equally firm detractor from the authority of the oral law and contributed significantly to its demise. Although Hillel and Jesus agreed on the centrality of the command to love God and man, they differed markedly on man's ability to actually do it. Although Hillel and Jesus both affirmed the Golden Rule, Jesus' positive statement of the rule was much more difficult to obey. And although Hillel and Jesus were known for their goodness, Jesus stated emphatically that true goodness belongs to God alone (Matthew 19:17).

How might Jesus approach you if you had a spiritual profile resembling that of Hillel and his followers? Here are several questions He might ask:

- Have you ever failed morally in a "big" way? How did it affect your relationship with God?
- Does your conscience ever caution you about fudging on God's truth, lowering God's standards, or extending God's permissions?

- What does love mean to you? How would you define and do you practice "tough love"?
- Honestly, what are the ways you try to justify yourself before God?
- When people praise your humility, what goes through your head?
- Would you say your spiritual life needs to be tweaked or radically transformed?
- How much confidence do you have in your ability to obey God's law?
- Are you as sensitive to sins of omission as sins of commission?
- Have you ever wanted to get out of the sin management business?
- Have you ever made a real fool of yourself, or been exposed as a real fool?
- In your pursuit of the good have you ever thought it's not good enough?
- How do you respond to being treated unfairly? Not receiving what you deserve?
- Does it ever gripe you to be overworked, overlooked, and underappreciated?
- Have you ever fudged the truth in order to forge the relationship?

WORK FOR JESUS

How might we be more useful in representing Jesus to people we meet who are Hillel-like in background and outlook? What can we learn from Jesus about how to reach those who try to please God and earn heaven by doing good?

1. Making a Connection

The connections between Jesus and the followers of Hillel were numerous and natural. They connected in homes, in the marketplace, in the synagogue, and the temple. They frequented the same places and traveled in similar circles, being orthodox Jews. So the opportunities for meaningful interaction were everywhere.

For those who find themselves resembling the spiritual profile of Hillel, connection with people will likely not be difficult. Generally those who possess a humble spirit, treat others with respect, follow the rules, and live right will not lack friends. And hopefully, those who follow in the footsteps of Jesus will have constant opportunities, as Jesus did, to connect with kindred spirits.

2. The Tone of the Conversation

The tone of most of Jesus' interactions with the Hillelites was probing and emotionally deep. It was, therefore, easy to understand each other and get on each other's nerves. Jesus' love for the followers of Hillel was strong. He gets mad when they don't get it, He's glad when they do, and He is sad when they walk away. I suspect that Jesus could and would reduce a sincere Hillelite to tears quickly with His probing questions, touching stories, and lofty standards.

Today many Christians harbor a stereotype about the Pharisees, labeling them "hypocrites," "Christ-killers," "self-righteous prudes," and a host of equally derogatory terms. Interestingly, in a first-century Jewish synagogue, they would range from "humble" and "loving" to "faithful to God." So which is it? I submit that the people in the synagogue are more correct than the people in church pews. Because we are ignorant of the different kinds of Pharisees, we tend to generalize too much.

In human relationships we usually say the strongest and harshest things to those we love the most. Thus in Jesus' interactions with the followers of Hillel, I sense His affection, feel His sadness, and see His tears for those He loves. When we read the Pharisees as scoundrels we seldom, if ever, see how much they resemble ourselves!

3. Finding Common Ground

The common ground Jesus shared with the followers of Hillel was continental. The resemblances are so many that it is no surprise that Jesus is widely considered to have been a disciple of Hillel Himself. The Hillelites' synthesis of the Old Testament, their exposition of the Golden Rule, their compassion, humility, and modesty, are all remarkably consistent with the teachings of Jesus. I suspect the Gospels include so many accounts of Jesus and the Pharisees because they shared so much in common. Moreover, it was the apostle Paul's wise strategy to go to the synagogue first in towns he visited because there he too found much common ground.

4. Losing the Found

Like the Samaritans and the Sadducees, the Hillelites thought they had found and were protecting true religion. After all, the Scriptures called them God's "chosen people." They celebrated the Feasts and offered the sacrifices, and they followed the law. Yet as compliant, law-abiding, compassionate, humble, and loving people, the Hillel Pharisees had self-righteousness subtly and unknowingly creep into their soul. The major method by which Jesus sought to get the Hillelites "lost" was by raising the bar of righteousness when He interacted with them.

Consider several of Jesus' statements in Matthew 5: anger is like murder, lust is like adultery, massaging the truth is malignant, be wronged rather than retaliate, love your enemies, and "be perfect, therefore, as your heavenly Father is perfect" (v. 48). Ironically Jesus is accused of abolishing the law when in fact He is faithfully defining and fulfilling it. At every turn with the Hillel Pharisees Jesus shows God's actual standards to be impossible to fulfill. And Jesus would readily add that the Pharisees' approach to God's law actually eviscerated it and diverted them from the righteousness God seeks.

5. Surprisingly . . .

What most surprises me about Jesus' interactions with the followers of Hillel is how radical Jesus is. I would have been far "kinder and gentler." After all, the followers of Hillel were good people, sensitive souls, teachable, and kind. Yet Jesus insisted on being "born again," that sins of omission were just as serious as sins of commission, and that nothing short of perfection was acceptable. The problem with the Pharisees' perspective was not minor in Jesus' eyes; it was of paramount importance.

6. Slogans and Symbols

Surveying the incidents and contexts in which Jesus interacts with the Hillel Pharisees, babies and children are often involved. Let me cite some examples. Jesus is still a child when He first interacts with the Pharisees (Luke 2:41–50). And when Jesus talks with Nicodemus, He suggests that Nicodemus must become a spiritual fetus in order to see the kingdom of God. Jairus comes to Jesus because of the need of his child. And the story of the Good Samaritan follows right on the heels of Jesus' praise of God's revealing the hidden things of the kingdom to "little children" (Luke 10:21). Even the story of the rich young ruler immediately follows Jesus' teaching about the kingdom and children. The greatest spiritual lessons Hillelites need to learn come from babies and children.

All parents realize their children are precious—but they are not innocent. They are innately selfish. They disobey, lie, steal, cover up, and blame-shift instinctively. And they do all of these things with so little sophistication. As adults, "good people" have learned to cover up much better, to blame more believably, to hide more effectively.

What is it, then, about babies and children that Hillelites need to see? Children are vulnerable, dependent, weak, and trusting—and babies are even more so.

7. Connecting with Jesus

Seeing Jesus as God's righteousness is the preeminent insight, and receiving Jesus as my righteousness is the preeminent work. Surely the Scripture-savvy Pharisees knew Isaiah 64:6, "All of us have become like one who is unclean, and all our righteous acts are like filthy rags." I wonder what they thought. We do know that a very famous Jew, schooled under one of Hillel's students, wrote the following:

But whatever was to my profit I now consider loss for the sake of Christ. What is more, I consider everything a loss compared to the surpassing greatness of knowing Christ Jesus my Lord, for whose sake I have lost all things. I consider them rubbish, that I may gain Christ and be found in him, not having a righteousness of my own that comes from the law, but that which is through faith in Christ—the righteousness that comes from God and is by faith. (Philippians 3:7–9)

He, the apostle Paul, connected with Jesus!

I conclude this chapter on the followers of Hillel with the words of detective Father Brown in G. K. Chesterton's *The Secret of Father Brown*:

No man's really any good till he knows how bad he is, or might be; till he's realized exactly how much right he has to all this snobbery, and sneering, and talking about "criminals," as if they were apes in a forest ten thousand miles away; till he's got rid of all the dirty self-deception of talking about low types and deficient skulls; till he's squeezed out of his soul the last drop of the oil of the Pharisees; till his only hope is somehow or other to have captured one criminal, and kept him safe and sane under his own hat.[6]

Profile:
The Shammai Pharisees

Whoever undertakes to set himself up as a judge of Truth and Knowledge is shipwrecked by the laughter of the gods.

—ALBERT EINSTEIN

7

JESUS *and the* TRUTH SEEKERS

Some years ago while teaching philosophy of religion at our local community college, I asked my class how they decided what was true. A woman spoke up and told the following story to the class. "Earlier this year my mother passed away. After the funeral service, while walking to the hearse with my father, his pants fell down all the way to his ankles."

The class and I started to chuckle and stare at her quizzically.

"And how," I asked, "did this event help you decide what was true?"

"In life my mother liked to perform practical jokes. And my confirmation that she was alive in the next world was that she pulled down Dad's pants." We stifled our laughter while she fought back tears.

For this student, truth can be known through personal experience. Truth in our society is being deconstructed, and religion is following suit. More than twenty years ago University of Chicago professor Allan Bloom wrote, "There is one thing a professor can be absolutely certain of: almost every student entering the university believes, or says he believes, that truth is relative."[1]

Nevertheless, people of all stripes still advocate for truth. We demand truth in advertising. Law courts require witnesses to take an oath to tell "the truth, the whole truth, and nothing but the truth." Former Vice President Al Gore stars in the award-winning documentary *An Inconvenient Truth*, and Focus on the Family produces *The Truth Project*. And Jack Nicholson's character in *A Few Good Men* mouths the famous line, "You can't handle the truth."

The spiritual profile in Jesus' day that was most convinced it could handle the truth was the Pharisees that followed Shammai, today's truth seekers. Let's meet their hero.

INTRODUCING SHAMMAI THE ELDER

Within the history of Judaism, Shammai the Elder stands out as a stickler for the truth of God's Word. From scant evidence we can glean that Shammai was born in Palestine around 50 BC and died approximately AD 30. These dates make him the contemporary of his antithetical counterpart, Hillel, and, interestingly, also Jesus of Nazareth. He worked as an engineer or surveyor in addition to his study and teaching of the Law.

Shammai studied Judaism under the great sages Shemaiah and Abtalion along with Hillel, his fellow student. Eventually Shammai began his own rabbinic academy. He entered the public stage of Israel after Menachem, a leader in the Jewish Sanhedrin, was recruited by King Herod for a government post. Shammai then became a leader of the ruling body of Israel.

The statements from and stories about Shammai paint him as a "no nonsense" leader who set high standards, obeyed them himself, and expected others to follow suit. He was passionate for the precise truth of God's law, arguing vehemently for what he thought was right. Though known to be stern, Shammai admonished his students to "receive all men with a cheerful countenance."[2] However, in various accounts of Shammai's dealings with potential students, he insisted on high standards. And when a potential recruit dissed the oral law, Shammai dismissed him summarily. Shammai apparently did not choose to waste his time with those who had a superficial commitment.

Shammai's strict adherence to the Law is well

documented by several rulings he issued and actions he took. These ranged from how to celebrate the Sabbath—strictly avoid all prohibited activities but celebrate the day with the best of everything—to what to do if you forget to say grace after a meal. In the case of forgotten grace, if you finish the day only to realize you did not thank God for your meal, you must go back to where you ate and say grace.

Shammai and his Sanhedrin counterpart, Hillel, agreed on all matters pertaining to orthodox Pharisee theology, but disagreed on numerous specific applications of law to life. They and their respective schools famously clashed on over three hundred specific applications of the law, including divorce, mezuzah placement on doorposts, lighting Hanukkah candles, offering sacrifices, celebrating feasts, paying tithes, obeying purity laws, and many more. They also disagreed on politics. Shammai, while not formally in the violence-advocating Zealot camp, certainly sympathized with their anti-Roman sentiments. Moreover, Shammai regarded separation from Gentiles and Jewish sinners necessary, while Hillel was more open. However, lest you think that the disagreements between Shammai and Hillel were worthless wrangling, the Mishnah states, "Any controversy that is for God's sake shall in the end be of lasting worth, but any that is not for God's sake shall not in the end be of lasting worth. Which controversy was for God's sake? Such was the controversy of Hillel and Shammai.

And which was not for God's sake? Such was the contro-versy of Korah and all his company."[3]

Shammai did, however, have a softer side (and so did his followers). In about a dozen debates with Hillel and his school, Shammai and his followers took the more lenient stand. These seemingly out-of-character stands are spe-cially noted in the Mishnah. And though Shammai insisted on a rigorous examination of truth, when he was shown to be in error he conceded.

During the life of Jesus and the apostles, Shammai and his followers were dominant in the religious life of Israel. After the destruction of Jerusalem and the temple in AD 70, Hillel's school became prominent in rabbinical circles and dominates the religious life of Judaism to this day.

TENDENCIES of the Shammai Pharisees

Truth: Truth for Shammai and his followers emanated from the character of God, as expressed in the law of Moses, and as literally interpreted and applied by the great rabbis in the oral law.

Economics: The Pharisees were the party of the people. They represented the working class, the man-on-the-street, and the average Joseph and Mary of Judaism in Jesus' day.

Neighborhood: The Pharisees' base of operations was the synagogue, the community center of Judaism. Being orthodox in theology, working-class economically, and conservative politically, the Shammaites enjoyed a good reputation and a strong sense of community.

Devotion: The word *obedience* best sums up Shammai's approach to the spiritual life. Obedience to God's law is mingled with mercy. Obedience to God's law is motivated by truth. And obedience to God's law is the path to life, not bondage.

Everyman: The Pharisees straddled the fine line between a strict belief in God's sovereignty and human freedom. Though God knows all, human choice is real and human choices matter.

Nature of God: The sentiments of the followers of Shammai toward God are reflected by King David, "Lord, who may dwell in your sanctuary? Who may live on your holy hill? He whose walk is blameless and who does what is righteous, who speaks the truth from his heart" (Psalm 15:1–2).

Civics: The Shammaites were political conservatives, just right of the Hillelites and just left of the Zealots. As nationalists they despised Roman taxation and rule. As patriots they sought freedom. And as separatists they would have preferred if all Gentiles would leave their land and "go home."

I*mmortality:* Human beings, according to the Shammaites, are immortal and their eternal destiny will be determined by their righteousness on earth. Some will go to heaven, some to hell, and some will require further refinement. Followers of Shammai seem to have believed in a resurrection body.

E*thics:* Right and wrong is determined by the commands of God as revealed in His law. The bumper sticker, "God said it, I believe it, that settles it," may have been popular among the Shammaites.

S*ummary:* The psalmist best sums up the Shammaites' worldview, "I have chosen the way of truth; I have set my heart on your laws" (Psalm 119:30).

WATCH JESUS

How did Jesus interact with the followers of Shammai in His day? Consider these eleven encounters.[4]

"Your Sins Are Forgiven"
(The "Discerning" Pharisees)

Orthodox spiritual profiles are highly sensitive to small deviations from bedrock scriptural truth. To the Pharisees, the most important command of God is the prohibition against blasphemy (Leviticus 24:10–16). Thus, the Pharisees immediately react when Jesus tells a man He had never met that his sins are forgiven (Matthew 9:1–8; Mark 2:1–12; Luke 5:17–26). I, and most people I know, most certainly would have joined their ranks. Jesus is either mega-arrogant or laughably crazy. Jesus, however, does not see discernment but heart disease beneath the Pharisees' response. What did the divine physician diagnose? Maybe Jesus sees how the plaque of a theological system has blocked them from being more curious about His identity. Maybe He notices a hole in their logic when He points out that it is much easier to say something ("I forgive your sins") than to do something (heal the man's paralysis). Maybe Jesus is perturbed that the well-documented fruit of His "medical practice" in the region has been discounted. When we watch Jesus at work with the Shammaites, we notice that He piously pokes holes in their truth system and hopes for a curious, rather than prejudiced, response.

Party at Matthew's House
(The "Healthy" Pharisees)

Table fellowship with the "impure" is particularly odious to Shammai and his followers. So when Jesus accepts a dinner invitation to Matthew the tax-collector's house, the Pharisees are suspicious (Matthew 9:9–13; Mark 2:13–17; Luke 5:27–32). Taxation without representation, collaboration with the Romans, and separation from sinners are all Shammaite hot-button issues. Jesus, however, views His involvement with Matthew and friends in a far different light. To Jesus, hanging out with the "sinners" perfectly coincides with His occupation as a soul doctor, His commitment to the priorities of God, and His mission in the world.

Jesus' tongue must have been protruding through His cheek when He "agrees" with the Pharisees' self-assessment that they were doing fine. They are "the healthy," Jesus says, and without need of a doctor (Luke 5:31). But since Jesus is a doctor He gravitates toward the sick, and since Jesus has a bias toward mercy He seeks out the miserable, and since Jesus was on a mission to save He looked for the unrighteous.

Clearly, the Pharisees don't need Jesus since they are spiritually healthy, happy, and holy! But the sick, struggling, sinners need and want Him. "I have not come to call the [so-called] righteous, but sinners to repentance," Jesus told the Pharisees (v. 32). When we watch Jesus at work among the Pharisees we notice that He selectively uses sarcasm to suggest that separatism may be counterproductive, and contrary to the purposes of God.

Healing on the Sabbath
(The Fencing Pharisees)

Fidelity to Sabbath law is a primary concern for the Pharisees, particularly Shammai and his followers. They see the Sabbath as specially set apart by God as the institution that defines them, protects them, strengthens them, and punishes them for disobedience. They esteem the Sabbath, noting that it is the longest of the Ten Commandments. It is referred to more than any other command in the written law, and accumulates more space in the oral law than any other single topic. The Sabbath is the focus of the Jewish faith, and the main law of God generating fences to keep people from breaking it. Thus, the conflicts between Jesus and the Pharisees over the Sabbath are pivotal, and early on became the basis for the plots to execute Jesus.

The Gospels record seven healings that Jesus performed on the Sabbath.[5] Five of these involve the Pharisees, and they have some features in common. Jesus does not know any of the people He heals. Nevertheless, He initiates the healings and incites a fight with the Pharisees. Jesus is accused of breaking the law, thus evoking the conclusion that He is not from God. Jesus counters that He is in lockstep with His Father, doing good on the Day, and ironically, consistent with the Pharisees own Sabbath permissions. The Pharisees don't buy Jesus' explanations. Instead they decide He has to go.

The give-and-take between the Pharisees and the formerly blind man (John 9) is the stuff of prime-time comedy. The blind guy becomes more and more confident in Jesus, while the Pharisees become more and more irritated and irrational. With one-liners, the blind man makes fools of the sighted. It is a classic case of one cool operator and a bunch of naysayers who lose their cool. What is ironic is that the expected roles are reversed. The blind man, probably without a lick of theological training, demonstrates formidable theological understanding, while those with much formal training in the law demonstrate formidable blindness. And this blindness is self-imposed.

When we watch Jesus in action with the Pharisees, we notice that He consistently prods them to take a deeper look at their "truths." Those whose profile parallels that of the followers of Shammai will often find themselves emotionally stirred—even to the point of hatred—when their cherished fences are trespassed.

Snacking on the Sabbath
(The Sabbath Sticklers)

When Jesus' disciples grab a snack of grain on the Sabbath, some Pharisees immediately detect a Sabbath violation (Matthew 12:1–14; Mark 2:23–3:6; Luke 6:1–11). The oral law that the Pharisees believe came from God defines work as consisting of thirty-nine specific activities.[6] The Shammaites are particularly strict about obeying them, but Jesus' disciples are not, violating at least four work restrictions as they snack that Sabbath.

With incredible economy of words, coupled with compelling logic, Jesus confronts the sticklers for truth. Jesus begins with the Old Testament, a source they all agree is authoritative, and points out God-allowed "violations" of Sabbath law. Jesus then quotes Hosea 6:6, identifying God's preference for human compassion over ritual purity. Additionally, Jesus highlights the inhuman conundrum that the oral law creates by allowing sheep to be pulled out of a pit on the Sabbath but prohibiting pulling a human being out of the pit of suffering on the Sabbath. The oral law is simply not acceptable to Jesus. He regarded it as man-made, inhumane, superficial, arbitrary, imprisoning, truth-twisting, and sometimes absurd.

The Pharisees have, by their penchant for fences, focused on don'ts. Jesus, with His penchant for freedom, focuses on dos. The Sabbath is a fine day for doing good. The Sabbath was never intended by God to place people in jail, but for man's good. It is a gift, not a punishment; an opportunity to trust God, not a duty to obey. And then Jesus delivers the coup de grace to the Sabbath—His supreme authority over it. Jesus called Himself "greater than the temple" and the "Lord of the Sabbath." When we watch Jesus at work with people passionate to protect their truth we notice that He cuts holes in their fences and beckons them to find freedom.

"Until Heaven and Earth Disappear"
(The "Righteous" Pharisees)

Jesus' violation of the principles of separation and His repeated breaking of the Sabbath categorize Him in the eyes of the Shammai Pharisees as a "liberal" with regard to the law. Jesus' first statement in the Sermon on the Mount about the law implies that He has been accused of ignoring the law (Matthew 5:17). In the strongest of terms Jesus affirms just the opposite; He not only sanctions every letter of the God's law but also lives every bit of it (vv. 17–20).

Where, then, is the disconnect? It's obvious! Jesus rejects the oral law, which to the Pharisees is tantamount to rejecting all God's law. Jesus makes a clear line of demarcation between God's written law (the Old Testament) and the Pharisees' oral law (tradition). In fact, Jesus seems to look for appropriate ways to violate the oral law. Why would He do this? Jesus regards the oral law as humanly authored (not divinely inspired), as humanly enabled (not divinely fulfilled by Christ), and as a route to nowhere (not the path of righteousness leading to the kingdom of heaven). When we watch Jesus at work with those who regard tradition as truth, we notice that He is sometimes ruthless because He alone realizes the spiritual subtractions that come from adding to God's Word.

"By Beelzebub"

(The Blaspheming Pharisees)

The tone and treatment of Jesus when He heals a man and is accused by the Pharisees of doing so by the power of Satan, seems Shammai-like (Matthew 12:22–45; Mark 3:23–30; Luke 11:14–32; cf. Matthew 9:34). When something ostensibly supernatural occurs, particularly when it involves demons, orthodox religious leaders are on the spot—they must provide a cogent explanation from Scripture—to the "faithful." And the stakes are raised considerably when the so-called miracle worker is suspect and the observers are increasingly impressed. So the Pharisees do two things: one, they attribute Jesus' powers to Satan, and two, they demand some substantiating proof of the source of the "miracle."

Those who make truth their highest value are forced to explain spiritual phenomena. Everything must fit into a theological box. In this case the options are limited: the healed man is a stooge, the "healer" is a phony, the power source is demonic, or the miracle comes from God. The man from whom the demons are exorcized is probably well known, thus not a stooge. The exorcism seems authentic, thus not a sham. And the Pharisees have already decided that Jesus is a lawbreaker, a Messianic pretender; thus God is not involved. That leaves only one explanation, Satan.

Jesus counters the truth brigade with some truth of

His own. First, Jesus points out the craziness of Satan (a demon) casting out demons. To do so would be akin to "shooting oneself in the foot." Satan is not stupid enough to attack himself. Second, the Pharisees claim that God can exorcise demons. So if Satan isn't involved, who is? Third, Jesus forces the Pharisees to ponder deeply the significance of His demon-destroying ministry. If Satan is not a logical source, nor is trickery involved, then God must have been at the core of what Jesus did. The kingdom of God has come, the stronger man has won, and decision-time has arrived. And for the sign-seekers, Jesus gives them what they asked for and hated, the ultimate sign— the "sign of Jonah." Jonah, given life after a sure death, preached repentance to a most wicked nation, the Assyrians, and they repented. And Jonah was a pip-squeak (not to mention also a rebellious prophet) in comparison to Jesus.

"So what will you do?" Jesus asks. When we watch Jesus at work with "champions of the truth," we notice that His miracles posed a challenge to those who insisted on thinking inside a man-made theological box.

Food Fight
(The Kosher Pharisees)

Food is one of the most interesting elements of religious observance. Almost all religions have laws governing foods, fasts, feasts, and especially, how to observe them properly. Judaism in Jesus' day not only included the kosher food laws (from the Mosaic law), but also various cleansing traditions (from the oral law). Jesus' followers didn't observe the cleansing traditions properly, so they were confronted by the Pharisees. Jesus uses the occasion to start a food fight and offer some profound food for thought on religious traditions (Matthew 15:1–20; Mark 7:1–23).

The oral law sought to make the written law of God understandable, measurable, and applicable. The motive for this pursuit was no doubt noble. However, religious traditions have an undercurrent that is unsuspectingly dangerous. Jesus, ever the guardian of God's truth, identifies this undercurrent in reference to the Pharisees' food and cleansing traditions. Jesus makes several stunning observations in this encounter with these "kosher" Pharisees. One, religious traditions have the ability to confer a sense of rightness without actual righteousness. Two, very quickly religious people lose sight of the fact that traditions are man-made, not God-given. Three, religious traditions may conflict with biblical theology, but the power of tradition readily rationalizes the conflict away. Four, religious traditions can even reverse the truth of God's Word. In fact, the Pharisees' hand-washing traditions had done precisely that. They taught that defilement comes from the outside in rather than from the inside out. Five, Jesus, the law's

Author and only fulfiller, "declared all foods 'clean'" (Mark 7:19).

When we watch Jesus at work among the law-multiplying Pharisees, we notice that He not only exposed the hidden dangers of religious tradition, but also the opportunities for self-discovery and ministry that they often thwart (cf. interaction with a Gentile woman in her home; Matthew 15:21–28; Mark 7:24–30).

"Get 'em"
(The Cocksure Pharisees)

John 7 is a watershed chapter in the opposition of the Pharisees to Jesus. Many of the themes that have been introduced earlier are brought to the table and thrashed out here. It begins with Jesus on the run for His life (v. 1) and ends with Him almost under arrest (v. 52). In between is recorded some most enlightening back-and-forth banter about who Jesus is. Is Jesus the Messiah? Is He good? Where did He get His smarts? (See vv. 2–5, 12, and 15, respectively.) Is He demon possessed? Why do the religious authorities hate Him so? What has He done wrong? Where does He come from? Where is He going? Is He the Prophet?[7] Where did He get His eloquence?

The questioning of the crowds is contrasted with the cocksureness of the religious leaders. The crowds are ambivalent about Jesus being the Messiah (vv. 25–27), while the leaders try to seize Him as a messianic pretender (v. 30). Many in the crowd believe Jesus (v. 31), while the religious leaders try to arrest Him (v. 32). The people are divided in their perception of Jesus' identity (vv. 41–44), while the religious leaders were dead set on theirs (v. 47). The "mob" of people are drawn to Jesus (vv. 46–48), while the religious leaders started swearing (v. 49). When we watch Jesus at work we notice that He constantly prodded people to wrestle with His true identity.

"God Is My Witness"
(The Judicial Pharisees)

John 8 seems to steal a page from a legal textbook. What begins with a woman accused of a capital crime, morphs into an exposé of corrupt judicial procedures, then into a debate about witnesses, and finally into a straightforward statement of Jesus' divine identity, resulting in another capital crime—blasphemy—supposedly being committed (v. 58). A peculiar conversation, full of twists and turns, begins with Jesus calling His Father and Himself to the "witness stand." From Jesus' perspective, there are no better witnesses in the entire world. From the Pharisees' perspective, however, Jesus' assertion opens a can of theological worms. And Jesus jumps right into the fray! He links Himself uniquely with the Father, asserts His home is in heaven, promises that His "lifting up" will substantiate His claims, states that His teaching was spiritually emancipating and would conquer death, and as a crowning conclusion called Himself "I Am."

Ten times in the dialogue of John 8 Jesus uses the word "truth." When we watch Jesus at work among the truth-seeking Pharisees, we notice that He, truth incarnate, will expose the truth in ways that will either enlighten or blind.

"Jesus Did Not First Wash before the Meal" (The Surprised Pharisee)

In a previous episode, Jesus' disciples were "caught" ignoring the cleansing requirements of the oral law.[8] Now Jesus is invited over to a Pharisee's house for dinner; there He is "caught" also ignoring the laws of hand cleansing (Luke 11:37–54). Rather than offer a rationale for His "transgression," Jesus pointedly addresses the deeper issue of spiritual superficiality, a common attribute of truth-seeking spiritual profiles. The Pharisees had reversed God's values, giving more weight to lesser priorities. Thus, they value measurable behaviors (like tithing) over a lifestyle of love and justice, recognition by man over the "Well done" of God, ritual cleanness over moral goodness, and head over heart. When we watch Jesus at work with those who pursue perfection, we notice that He was relentless in pushing the envelope.

Money Lovers
(The Materialistic Pharisees)

Orthodox spiritual profiles can develop extraordinary skill in redefining sins they like, materialism being a common example. Making money is normally attributed to hard work, virtuous living, good stewardship, and God's blessing. And in large measure these are true. However, with accumulating assets (or even without them) materialism is one of those sins that is easy to ignore, justify, and even religiously reinforce. In my Bible, a red-letter version that identifies when Jesus is speaking, there is a single sentence in black in Luke 16, "The Pharisees, who loved money, heard all this and were sneering at Jesus" (v. 14). The rest of the chapter is devoted by Dr. Luke to Jesus' instructions on money in parables and exhortations.

The Pharisees are hardworking, law-abiding, wise-living, and God-honoring. Thus, they normally did all right financially—just as such people often do today. A common unintended and often unacknowledged consequence of good financial management is materialism. And apparently the Pharisees have the disease and don't know it. But Jesus sees and confronts it. First, He tells the strange parable of the shrewd manager (16:1–9) to His disciples, and then draws some implications from it (vv. 10–13). These words of Jesus about wise stewardship of wealth and the tendency of money to become a master evoke the "sneering" of the Pharisees. Perhaps they wondered what this Galilean peasant without property knew about money. Maybe the Pharisees knew that a bunch of women were paying the bills for Jesus and His ragtag disciples (Luke 8:1–3). Probably they didn't get the message that money is a great test of both stewardship and worship.

Jesus ends His exposé of the Pharisees' love affair with money by telling the parable of the rich man and Lazarus (Luke 16:19–31). Jesus wants the Pharisees to see themselves as the rich man. With brilliant brush strokes, Jesus paints the rich man's luxurious life, his paltry generosity, his demise in hades, his longing for relief from the turn of tables he is experiencing in the afterlife, and his request to warn his still-living family. No, Jesus implies. If people do not "get it" from the teachings of Moses and the Prophets, they would not "get it" even if someone rose from the dead (as Lazarus and Jesus soon would do).

Living a good life ethically often leads to living a good life financially, which often leads to a sense of living a good life spiritually. Subtly sinister spiritual enemies sneak in. Money becomes more valuable than it actually is. Personal worth starts to be measured by net worth. Works start to replace grace. Contentment with tithing undermines open-handed generosity. Care for the poor easily degenerates into contempt for the lazy. When we watch Jesus at work with the Pharisees notice that He addressed money matters in ways that make them squirm—or see.

WALK WITH JESUS

How might Jesus talk with us if we had the opportunity to walk with Him? As with the ancient Shammai Pharisees, Jesus surely would want to highlight with truth seekers much that is commendable. Truth is very important to God, primarily because He is truth. The Pharisees regarded obeying God as a huge part of their covenantal responsibility. So, to identify God's commands from Holy Scripture, interpret them properly, illustrate them so that they are understandable to the common person, and then fence the law so that God's people won't break it was motivated by a deep reverence for God. Moreover, Jesus would likely applaud the commitment and courage it takes to stand for truth in a world that neither acknowledges nor practices it. The Shammaites were willing to take the flack that came their way for being sticklers for truth and principle. They believed in tough love, not enabling. Nor were they afraid to be countercultural. The faith "once delivered to the saints" was given by God to test hearts not tickle ears, to build character not appeal to consumers, and to produce holiness not happiness. There is a lot to love about people who work very hard to be right before God.

No doubt Jesus would also address some characteristic flaws of those who pursue truth as their highest value. First and foremost Jesus would want to differentiate between God's truth and man's. Having two truths inevitably results in contradictions, which Jesus was quick to point out to the Shammaites. Moreover, when encapsulating the "truth" into an "obeyable" system is the goal, it is inevitable that selective inclusion and omission of God's truth will occur in order to make everything fit. There is the tendency to create systems of thought and theology that do not entirely square with the whole counsel of God's Word. But to make facts fit, passages are sometimes ignored, truths are exaggerated, and contrary ideas are eliminated. And when the practice of "fencing the law" starts, it can never end. And over time the rules tend to become more and more absurd.

So, what questions might Jesus want to ask you if you possess a spiritual profile like that of Shammai and his followers—a would-be truth seeker?

- Do you judge yourself with the same criteria you use to judge others?
- Which do you do more naturally, tell people what to do or help them do what they should do?
- Is separation from "sinners" a big emphasis for you? What has it accomplished for you? What has it accomplished for "them"?

- Do you ever feel like a spiritual failure? If you do, what do you do with that feeling?
- How do you respond to theological assertions that do not fit your grid? Do they ever give you pause and make you uneasy?
- How do you discern what is truth and what is not?
- Have you encountered any disjunctions between your rules and God's Word? If so, how do you handle these?
- How does it feel when you encounter unfairness?
- Have you ever detected seeds of materialism growing in your soul?
- How do you respond when your truth is challenged?
- Honestly, how much anger is within you? Have you ever pondered what fuels it?
- How do you handle it when you are shown to be wrong? To be right?
- Has your quest for letter-perfect accuracy ever caused you to lose sight of the spirit of the law?

WORK FOR JESUS

How might we be more useful and effective in representing Jesus to people we meet who are Shammai-like in background and outlook? Here are seven areas to consider as you interact with truth seekers.

1. Making a Connection

Interestingly, many of the interactions I have identified as involving Jesus and the followers of Shammai have some connection with a "house." The "houses" include Simon Peter's house, Matthew's house, various Pharisees' houses, the "house of study" (synagogue), and "My Father's house" (the temple and its environs). What a fitting place for Jesus to connect with the truth seekers. A home is a place where we "let our hair down" and where the "rubber meets the road." We feel safe to speak our mind—and hopefully listen to others—in a home. One's house is the best place to wrestle with truth.

The book of Acts tells us that Paul the missionary characteristically went first to the synagogue of the towns he visited to share the good news about Jesus (13:14; 14:1; 17:1–2, 10; 18:4, 19; 19:8). He did this because of His conviction to bring the Gospel first to the Jews and then to the Gentiles. But I also suspect he did this because the synagogues were a venue where people took God's Word seriously, pondered it, preached it, sought to synthesize it, and most importantly live it in their daily lives. What better place to connect with truth seekers than where they gather to discuss truth. While it is true that both Jesus and Paul encountered substantial opposition while talking truth in the synagogue and temple, they at least were able to have a conversation there. Truth flourishes best where people can wrestle with it in an environment they find familiar. Jesus' representatives make "house calls."

2. The Tone of the Conversation

Almost every conversation between Jesus and the followers of Shammai is laced with questions. The tone, therefore, is quizzical. How appropriate that the man called truth (John 14:6) asked penetrating questions to the primary seekers of truth in His world. Occasionally, but not often, Jesus instructed or corrected the truth-seeking Shammaites. Usually He sought to penetrate their hearts with pertinent questions.

In many ways the Shammaites of old resemble journalists today. Both prided themselves on their objective quest for truth, but failed to adequately account for the ideological agenda that colored their perspective. Time and again they tracked Jesus down looking for a scoop. They asked questions designed to catch Him in a conundrum or get Him to misspeak. They were highly perturbed when their "fans" seemed to "fall" for the "imposter" from Nazareth. However, rather than give the Pharisees the interviews that they wanted, Jesus turned the tables and interviewed them! Asking wise (not trick) questions emanating from a loving (not critical) heart was Jesus' way to approach truth-loving Shammaites.

3. Finding Common Ground

The One who is "full of grace and truth" (John 1:14), who calls Himself "the way and the truth and the life" (John 14:6), and who says His true disciples "will know the truth, and the truth will set you free" (John 8:31–32), occupied abundant common ground with those whose highest value is finding and following the truth. Seventy-eight times the phrase "I tell you the truth" appears in the Gospels. The common ground Jesus shared—and shares—with Shammaites is the Word of God. Today's truth seekers may have a slightly different corpus of truth and interpretation thereof, yet I have found uniform deference to the authority of God's Word. This provides a common constitution from which to build a case, a sanctioned referee— the Bible—to arbitrate disputes, and a healthy dose of mystery to produce humility.

4. Losing the Found

Those who passionately pursue truth and are quite convinced that they have found it, are rather hard to get lost! They may feel little need to discover something they believe they already have. What did Jesus do to try to get those passionate for truth sufficiently lost that they seek the Way? I found Him doing three things. First Jesus made shocking statements designed to disarm the Pharisees. "Your sins are forgiven" (Matthew 9:2) and "You belong to your father, the devil" (John 8:44) and "It is not the healthy who need a doctor" (Matthew 9:12) and many more one-liners must have turned heads, and hopefully provoked introspection. Second, Jesus committed unacceptable acts designed to provoke thought and poke holes in the Pharisees' system. Accordingly, He purposely busted the Pharisees' Sabbath fences and broke their cleansing traditions. Third, Jesus straightforwardly stated His identity. He called Himself the sin-forgiver, the law-fulfiller, greater-than-the-temple, the "Lord of the Sabbath," the "I Am," the Messiah, and "one with the Father." The Pharisees could— and did—reject Jesus the Truth, but they could not say they did not give informed consent.

5. Surprisingly . . .

Two things surprised me about Jesus' interactions with the Shammaite Pharisees. First, Jesus seemed to have provoked them, purposely picking fights. Jesus instigated Sabbath squabbles, started food fights, and went to war over hand washings. Jesus claimed to forgive sins and called them sons of the Devil. Why was Jesus so in-your-face with the Pharisees? Second, Jesus seemed to use the word "hypocrite" most often with this particular spiritual profile. Few words are more distasteful to religious people than being called a hypocrite. People who make no claim to follow the truth can live diabolical lives and not be labeled a hypocrite.

But those who make claims to follow the truth, and then live inconsistently with it, are immediately dubbed hypocrites.

Hypocrisy is a label, therefore, that is largely affixed only on those who "ask for it." If Jesus came back to earth today, I think it's likely that we who most pride ourselves as "people of the Book" would be most likely to have our hypocrisy exposed.

6. Slogans and Symbols

While visiting Israel several years ago, I asked a Jewish man what he thought about Jesus. His response was succinct: "What you Christians believe about Jesus is unthinkable to a Jew. We don't even have the mental categories to comprehend it." Clearly Jesus didn't—and doesn't—fit the religious box that the Pharisees—ancient and modern—have created. To understand Jesus, no matter what religious background one comes from, requires "thinking outside the box," as Apple Computer reminds us.

The theological box that the Shammaites had created was formidable. They sought to cull out every commandment, fence every law, formulize every ritual, and develop a body of tradition that perfectly embodied God's timeless truth. They did not want to leave living the spiritual life to the wolves of error or compromise. And they fully expected that the much-anticipated Messiah would fall in lockstep with them.

And then came Jesus of Nazareth. He could not have been more "outside their box." Persistently and passionately, Jesus goaded them to think differently. For if they couldn't, or wouldn't, their spiritual destiny was in jeopardy. So Jesus identified the loopholes and criticized the contradictions and highlighted the verses they had "conveniently" omitted. Then He picked apart their traditions and busted their fences and provoked emotional reactions so as to prod them to reevaluate their conclusions. Adding insight to injury Jesus constantly dropped clues as to His identity and highlighted the mysteries of God and provided numerous puzzle pieces confirming that He was indeed the Messiah. Relentlessly Jesus prodded, provoked, and pushed the Pharisees to wrestle with a new theological reality. And I submit that a fair reading of the Gospels today by truth seekers would arouse a similar reaction—but hopefully different results.

7. Connecting with Jesus

The ultimate question Jesus wanted every spiritual profile to consider was His identity. With each, Jesus tailored His self-revelation to His specific audience. Jesus, "the truth," was the facet that He most wanted the Shammaites to grasp. Thus, Jesus first vehemently attacked the Pharisees' source of truth, an amalgam of human reasoning and divine revelation. Then, He criticized their theological "math"—they had added to the Scriptures, subtracted verses that didn't fit their system, multiplied rules and regulations, and failed in "rightly dividing the word of truth" (2 Timothy 2:15).

Finally, Jesus consistently goaded them to realize that truth is not a what, but a who, not a set of propositions, but a Person. That is what He does today with every sincere truth seeker.

Profile:
The Zealots

Politics is the art of looking for trouble, finding it everywhere, diagnosing it incorrectly and applying the wrong remedies.

—GROUCHO MARX

8

JESUS *and the* PASSIONATE ONES

Political passions run deep and wild. Among churchgoers, politics generates more emotion, polarization, and potential for disunity than any other issue (except perhaps worship style). How do I know? It's rather easy to detect. Notice what lights up the eyes, quickens the tempo, and raises the pitch of the voice, and dominates the conversation. Feel the heat.

When it comes to politics, emotion pours out of our pores. Listen to the words. Otherwise reasonable people seem to lose a measure of objectivity, use loaded words, take cheap shots, resort to exaggeration, and place on scapegoats absurd accusations. And by the way, I find this passion for politics to infect both sides of the political aisle equally.

Politics are obviously important, or they wouldn't generate such emotion and attention. The decisions of our political leaders do affect our lives in profound and practical ways. They play a pivotal role in our sense of peace and security, our notions of justice and fairness, our pursuit of happiness, our definitions of right and wrong, the saving and taking of human life, and "most important of all" our pocketbooks.

There is nothing fundamentally wrong with possessing a passion for politics. However, the imbalances that this passion can produce should give us pause. What if people feel more deeply about their ideology than their theology? What if political passions overshadow theological principles? What if passion for a candidate exceeds passion for Christ? What if politics trumps spirituality?

Not only do churches tend to divide over political passion, politics also frequently degenerates conversations, increases suspicion, fuels self-righteousness, promotes infighting, and demeans people. As noted above, political solutions often are viewed as more important than scriptural ones, so that at times political principles usurp biblical values.

In Jesus' day those whose politics dominated their theology were the Zealots.[1] The Zealots were orthodox in theology, readily joining the ranks of the Pharisees in their beliefs. In fact, they would have been in complete agreement with the Pharisees' doctrinal statement. But it was not doctrine that distinguished them—it was the passion, the practice, and the power of their political ideology that defined them. The Zealots eschewed the political passivity of so many of their theological compatriots; they refused to live like timid pansies accepting Roman domination and infiltration of their culture. Indeed, as a last resort they would endorse violence as an acceptable means to their end of freedom to worship their God as they believed. Though the main targets of their political zeal were the Romans, they also assailed their fellow Jews, who they perceived to be too soft or accommodating on Roman occupation. But that's getting ahead of ourselves. Let's go back and consider some history.

zealots AND THE ZEALOTS

Those zealots[2] active in Jesus' day looked to Phinehas as their original hero. The people of Israel had encountered the Moabites en route to the Promised Land (Numbers 22–25). The Moabites realized they could not withstand the Israelite juggernaut, so instead of fighting or surrendering, the Moabites opted for divination (through Balaam) and then seduction (through Baal-worship). It worked!

Seduced by the Moabites, the Israelites participated in significant immorality and idolatry. Eventually a plague of judgment broke out, and Moses commanded the leaders of the people to put to death the instigators. In a move designed for maximum publicity, however, a Jew named Zimri flaunted his rebellion against God with a Midianite woman named Cozbi by parading into their tent. Phinehas was outraged. He grabbed a spear, entered the tent where the couple were cavorting, and ran them through. The plague was stopped, Phinehas was hailed for his zeal and richly rewarded (25:6–15). Phinehas thus became the "gold standard" of zeal among the Jewish people.

Zeal for God (His law, His land, His lordship) remained part of the Jewish experience, from Phinehas in the second millennium before Christ to the Jewish underground group Haganah in the second millennium AD. The Old Testament praises the zeal of God[3] and the zeal of God's people.[4] It also warns about zeal gone awry (Proverbs 19:2).

Around the time of Jesus' birth, in the area of His childhood, Jewish resentment against Roman rule grew nasty. Some Jewish patriots attacked Roman positions and were brutally punished for their rebellion. During the public ministry of Jesus, Roman rule was unpopular among most of the Jews. So zealous patriots operated as an underground movement, carrying out acts of thievery and murder against

Romans and perceived Roman sympathizers. They saw God alone as their king ("No Master but God" was their motto) and Roman taxation as unlawful, and refused to take on the yoke of "slavery" to Rome.

INTRODUCING
THE ZEALOTS

The semiofficial Zealot movement began in AD 6 in Galilee and came to a defiant end in AD 73 at Masada. In AD 6, Judas the Galilean (mentioned in Acts 5:37), led a revolt against a taxation scheme of Coponius the Roman governor. Although his uprising failed, the passions he aroused and the methods he advocated continued in the Zealots.

During the early days of the Christian church, under the emperorship of Caligula (37–41), Zealot passions were seriously aroused when the emperor ordered that a statue of himself be erected in the Jewish temple. Although Caligula was killed before the actual statue was erected, the fire of political opposition to Rome was fueled. And during the governorship of Felix (52–58), the Zealots were particularly active (cf. Acts 21:38).

The Zealots become a formidable force in the 60s (around the time of the martyrdom of the apostles Peter and Paul). The abuse of power, greed, and injustice of the

Roman leadership in Israel aroused the Zealots to take matters into their own hands. A particularly violent wing of the Zealots was called the *Sicarii* (Latin for "violent men"). They received this name from their practice of hiding small daggers (*sicae*) under their clothes and stabbing people in crowds, sometimes fellow Jews who they thought were too friendly with the Romans. Josephus highlights the Zealots' passion, writing, "These men agree in all other things with the Pharisaic notions; but they have an inviolable attachment to liberty, and say that God is to be their only Ruler and Lord. They also do not count the cost of dying any kinds of death, nor indeed do they heed the deaths of their relations and friends, nor can any such fear make them call any man lord."[5]

The Zealots played a leading role in the Great Jewish Revolt (66–73). The revolt was precipitated by various Jewish grievances against the Roman occupiers and Roman frustration with Jewish random violence.[6] After the Roman legions defeated the Zealots in Galilee, the Zealots fled to the fortified city of Jerusalem. There they established their brutal authority, destroying food supplies and killing those who advocated surrender to the Romans. Eventually the Roman army under General Titus crushed Jewish resistance, burned Jerusalem, and demolished Herod's magnificent temple.

Some of the Zealots and their families then fled to

Masada, an impregnable mountain fortress built by para-
noid Herod the Great in the desert overlooking the Dead
Sea. At considerable cost and effort, the Roman army,
under the command of Lucius Flavius Silva, surrounded the
mountain, built a siege ramp, and in AD 73 breached the
walls of the fortress. When the Romans entered the fortress
they discovered that the almost one thousand Jewish inhabitants had committed mass suicide rather than submit to the
Romans. Thus the Zealots came to a bloody end on the top
of Masada. Almost two thousand years later, many Israeli
Defense Force recruits of the State of Israel climb the
ancient mountain fortress and declare "Masada Shall Not
Fall Again."

In the Jewish Talmud there is an interaction discussing
why the second temple was destroyed in AD 70:

Why was the first Sanctuary destroyed? Because of
three [evil] things which prevailed there: idolatry,
immorality, bloodshed. . . . But why was the second
Sanctuary destroyed, seeing that in its time they were
occupying themselves with Torah, [observance of] pre-
cepts, and the practice of charity? Because therein prevailed hatred without cause. That teaches you that
groundless hatred is considered as of even gravity with
the three sins of idolatry, immorality, and bloodshed
together.[7]

Thus, according to the rabbis, the Zealots were largely responsible for the demise of the nation of Israel.

TENDENCIES of The Zealots

Truth: Like the Pharisees, the Zealots officially acknowledged the written law (Torah) and the oral law (Mishnah) as their twin sources of truth. Unofficially, however, their political ideology, emphasizing autonomy and action, motivated them. So you might say that zealots, in general, have three sources of truth: the Book, or Scripture; their religious culture, or tradition; and their political beliefs, i.e., their ideology. Theoretically the sources would appear in this priority order, but practically the priority order is reversed—ideology trumps theology.

Economics: Zealots represent all socioeconomic classes. They may come from wealth, but they choose to devote their means to the cause. They may be well educated, but they despise those who substitute theory for action. They generally are pious, but they don't regard simply being nice as a virtue. They may be members of the community in good standing, but they do not tolerate compromise.

Neighborhood: The Zealots were members in good standing of the orthodox Jewish community. They regularly attended synagogue services. However, their real friends in the religious community were those who shared their political beliefs and passion.

Devotion: The Zealots took their spiritual life seriously and practically. Following God is all about following, not thinking, intending, or merely feeling. The spiritual life is about passion, action, obedience, courage, commitment.

Everyman: The Zealots viewed human beings as able to choose, and be responsible for their choices and actions. Since zealots emphasize passion and action, they most respect human beings who think ideologically, feel passionately, and act decisively. Zealots have contempt for those who are indifferent to their cause, or worse, seek their own comfort over the cause.

Nature of God: The Zealots maintained an orthodox Jewish view of God, emphasizing His jealousy.

Civics: The Zealots' politics defined them. They saw themselves as patriots, freedom fighters, and champions of Jewish autonomy in their land. They were opposed to the use of the Greek language, resented Roman intrusion into their high priesthood, despised paying taxes to the pagan Roman government, and longed for their (political) Messiah. And they advocated violence to achieve their ends. Basically, the Zealots were passionate about politics—their way!

Immortality: Just like the Pharisees, the Zealots believed in an afterlife, merited by those who actively, passionately, and courageously followed the law of God.

Ethics: The Zealots sought to follow the law of God themselves and compel others to do likewise. If they would not, the Zealots were not averse from engaging in uncivil disobedience, specifically violence. Their ethical system was based on a deep sense of loyalty to God's law coupled with an embrace of "the means justify in the end" thinking.

Summary: The Zealots would not settle for heterodoxy, mediocrity, indifference, cowardice, or political compromise, even from those who agreed with them theologically. They saw the state as a great enemy of the kingdom of God and were willing to throw their lot in with those who actively sought to overthrow and replace it. Thus they admired the likes of the Maccabees, those who fought for freedom.

WATCH JESUS

How did Jesus interact with the Zealots in His day? Consider these five encounters.

Divided Loyalties
(Simon the Zealot)

One of the carefully and prayerfully selected members of Jesus' disciples was "Simon the Zealot." Simon is mentioned just four times in the New Testament,[8] so we have very little data to understand him. However, a few things can be gleaned: First, Simon is called by two different names in the four accounts, "the Canaanite" and "the Zealot." Both names identify him either officially or unofficially with Jewish zealotry. Two, Simon is the only disciple whose political affiliation is mentioned. The closest the Scriptures come to matching this is identifying Matthew by his occupation, a tax collector. Third, Simon is listed toward the end; on two occasions his name appears next to Judas. Why? Perhaps Simon is a minor character among the Twelve, or maybe he shared some things in common with Judas. Nevertheless, like the other eleven, Simon was called by Jesus, to spend three years with Him, and to be sent out to represent Him (Mark 3:14).

The Gospels offer limited information about Simon the Zealot. Nevertheless, noting his political bent, some interesting questions arise: How did Simon the Zealot get along with Matthew the Herodian? Did Simon cringe when Jesus, in the Sermon on the Mount, explicitly proffered a message of nonretaliation (Matthew 5:38–42) and love for enemies (vv. 43–48)? How did Simon the Zealot respond when Jesus healed a Roman centurion's servant (8:5–13)? Did Simon wrestle with the increasingly clear fact that Jesus would not lead a rebellion against Rome? Why is a man known to be an activist so seemingly passive? What connections did Simon draw between Phinehas's disdain for immorality and Jesus' hanging out with the immoral? How did Simon like Jesus' response to the Herodians and Pharisees regarding the matter of paying taxes to Rome (Matthew 22:15–22; Mark 12:13–17; Luke 20:20–26)?

All those questions aside, what was Jesus doing? Why did Jesus pick Simon? Obviously Jesus was not averse to political differences, or differences in general. If He had been He would never have selected Matthew, a Roman collaborator, and Simon, a Roman collaborator-killer, to be His disciples! Jesus was pro-diversity. Maybe Jesus was trying to show that political ideologies pale in comparison to kingdom priorities. Maybe Jesus knew that the best way to impact a zealot is up-close-and-personal. Maybe Jesus picked Simon because Jesus liked activists who said little and did much. Jesus liked risk-takers, people of daring, people who seize the day, people of passion, hot-blooded people. Perhaps Jesus knew that a passionate zealot set on the right track is a powerful instrument for good.

Jesus also may have picked Simon because the two had some things in common. No doubt Simon was impressed by Jesus' zeal for God's house (John 2:13–22; Matthew 21:12–16; Mark 11:15–18; Luke 19:45–47). Simon probably was impressed by the fiery prophet from Galilee who stood toe-to-toe with the religious compromisers and hypocrites. I'll bet Simon saw in Jesus, as the other disciples also did, a would-be political Messiah who would free Israel from Rome's political and spiritual bondage. Some have even suggested that Jesus was a zealot.

When we watch Jesus at work with Simon the Zealot we notice three things. One, Jesus called him. This conveyed honor and acceptance. Two, Jesus gave Simon time to watch a true revolutionary at work. Political passions are not redirected quickly or easily. Finally, Jesus gave Simon an outlet for his passion that infinitely exceeded in importance and impact his political passions. Jesus gave Simon a new kingdom to which to devote himself. Jesus was trying to communicate that political ideology is not nearly as important as theology, nation building is not nearly as important as kingdom building, and political liberty is not as important as spiritual liberty. Tradition tells us that Simon the Zealot, like his Lord, died by crucifixion. I think he got it!

Judas the Traitor
(Judas)

The word *traitor* is primarily a political term. It brings to mind names like Brutus, Guy Fawkes, Benedict Arnold, Julius Rosenberg, Vidkun Quisling, Tokyo Rose, and Robert Hanssen. But first on every list of traitors is Judas Iscariot!

A case can be made, from Scripture and pseudo-scripture (e.g., the Gnostic *Gospel of Judas*), that Judas had Zealot political leanings. Judas's name likely indicates his hometown, Kerioth, though some suggest it could be connected with a branch of the Zealots. Perhaps Judas was an ardent nationalist who thought that Jesus would be, should be, and could be the leader who broke the bonds of Rome. Perhaps Judas started to get an inkling that a political messiah was not in the works. Maybe Judas thought he could force Jesus to come out as king, or stop Him. In either case, politics was a motivation. Once Judas left the kingdom of the King for the kingdom of the "prince" (John 12:31; 14:30; 16:11), his main collaborators were politicians (Matthew 26:14–16; Mark 14:10–11; Luke 22:3–6).

The reactions to Jesus' announcement of a betrayer in the upper room just hours before Jesus' arrest would be almost humorous if it were not so sobering (Matthew 26:20–25; Mark 14:17–21; John 13:18–30). The disciples, portraying considerable humility, suspect themselves instead of fingering anyone else. Jesus finally ends the speculation by identifying Judas as the traitor. Judas exits into the night. Stunningly, the remaining eleven wonder why Judas left. In this rare case, the traitor was able to "fool all the people all the time." The disciples were entirely unaware of Judas's hardened heart, his thievery, his satanic leanings, and his clandestine meetings.

Jesus' treatment of Judas is phenomenal. Jesus selected Judas to be among the Twelve. Then Judas was given the trusted task of handling the group's finances. Jesus let Judas in on the secrets of the kingdom (Matthew 13:11; Luke

8:10), knowing fully what Judas was up to in the secret places of his heart and the secret meetings with the Jewish leadership. Jesus never blew Judas's cover though Jesus did confront Judas where appropriate (John 12:1–8). On the night before His death, Jesus washed Judas's feet (John 13:1–17), gave Judas the place of honor at the Last Supper, and in an act of loyalty and friendship, dipped bread with Judas (Matthew 26:23; John 13:26). Jesus even called Judas "Friend" as Judas was betraying Him (Matthew 26:50). Jesus took pains to reach out to Judas to the very end. But once Judas had sold his soul to the Devil, and perhaps his heart to his political ideology, there was nothing Jesus could say or do to dissuade him. Such is the diabolical power of political passion gone to seed.

When we watch Jesus at work with Judas, we notice His long-suffering love. It seems as if Jesus went out of His way to include, honor, respect, teach, guide, caution, and protect Judas. Though Judas never genuinely responded to Christ's love, it can never be said that Jesus didn't try.

"Son of the Father"
(Barabbas)

Barabbas is a shadowy yet important character in the crucifixion story. We know very little about him except his name, his crime, and his surprise release. Barabbas's name may be significant. Literally his name means "Son of the father" or "Son of the rabbi." Possibly Barabbas was the son of a prominent rabbi. Barabbas's crime tells us that he was a Zealot. Matthew calls him a "notorious prisoner" (27:16), Mark and Luke cite Barabbas for insurrection and murder (Mark 15:7; Luke 23:19). Likely Barabbas was a leader of a band of "terrorists" who used thievery and murder to accomplish their political goals. And in a totally unexpected stroke of "luck," insurrectionist Barabbas is set free and "seditious" Jesus took his place on the cross (Luke 23:13-25; John 18:38-40).

No one knows what Barabbas thought about being set free, though a murderer, and watching an innocent man placed on "his" cross. Perhaps he simply dismissed it as a stroke of dumb luck. Perhaps he thought that someone in high places (maybe his father) had struck a deal. Perhaps he thought that this Jesus fellow was some poor sap. Or perhaps he thought long and hard about the man who took his spot at the "Place of the Skull" (Matthew 27:33). I wonder if the "son of the father" and the Son of the Father ever locked eyes or spoke words. Whatever Barabbas's other feelings, I can hardly imagine a heart so cold and hard not to wonder about this Jesus who died in his place. Sometimes it takes the sight of blood and guts and massive injustice to grab the attention of a zealot. And Jesus was willing to pay that price.

In many movie portrayals I have seen, Barabbas is pictured as an ugly, unkempt, dumb thug. In reality he may well have been handsome, educated, sophisticated, and religious. We like to paint our prisoners in dark hues, perhaps because they usually do their dirty work in the dark. However, with political zealots, the dark colors may not be altogether accurate, past or present. Many passionate political zealot revolutionaries come from relatively stable and middle- to upper-class backgrounds.[9] When we paint zealots as thugs, we fail to see who they really are, what drives them—or how to reach them.

Over the past decade our world has been shocked by the number of suicide bombings, which seem (and may in fact be) a daily occurrence. The popular notion is that the suicide bombers are hopeless, poor, disadvantaged, down-on-their-luck, uneducated, lowlifes. Why would anyone with a future so violently blow themselves up and with them many innocent victims? The answer is ideology and radical theology! Political ideology is a cause that regularly competes with Christ for the souls of men and women.

"Remember Me"
(The Thieves on the Cross)

Surely one of the most touching moments on the cross was when Jesus interacted with his cross mates, two "thieves" on either side of the Christ (Matthew 27:38; Mark 15:27; Luke 23:32–43). Some refer to the one who respected Jesus and asked for His intervention as "the thief who stole paradise." Jesus' cross mates may have been thieves, but not in the normal sense. In all likelihood they were insurrectionists, not common criminals.

Harmonizing the accounts of the crucifixion in the Gospels, it is apparent that one of the zealots on the cross with Jesus had a change of heart before his death. What changed? Perhaps it was the stark realization of his imminent death that sobered him. Maybe it was watching Jesus die. The "thief" saw Jesus' innocence (as opposed to his own guilt), Jesus' selflessness (as opposed to his comrade's self-centeredness), and Jesus' complete command of His destiny (as opposed to his own impotence). He believed Jesus' ability to offer salvation (although he simply hoped to be remembered). Jesus drew the thief close to steal his heart. That day, ironically, Jesus marched into paradise with a zealot. Jesus' love for a political ideologue was never more touchingly displayed.

When we watch Jesus at work with the thief on the cross, we notice Christ's exemplary humility and tenderness to the humble. One of the telling troubles of the politically passionate is the extent to which they see fault in others and miss it in themselves. Jesus offers an immediate ticket to heaven to a zealot who saw his own sin and turned to the Savior.

Zealous Persecutor Turned Preacher
(Saul of Tarsus)

If Phinehas was the Old Testament gold standard of zealotry, and the Maccabees were the intertestamental period exemplars of zealotry, and Judas the Galilean was the official founder of the Zealots, then Saul of Tarsus was the New Testament model of the heart and behavior of a zealot.

We first meet Saul at the martyrdom of Stephen (Acts 7:1–8:1). There as a young man he seemed to have been in the official position of approving authority as Stephen was executed. We know, from Paul's own testimony (Galatians 1:14 and Philippians 3:6), that as Saul his religious zealotry was legendary. But it seems that his religious zeal morphed into political zeal when he went on an authorized rampage to arrest and persecute Christians (Acts 8:3).

Saul seems to have been a zealot in all he did. He was zealous in his studies under Gamaliel (Acts 22:3). He was zealous for the law (Philippians 3:5). He was zealous in his persecution of Christians (Acts 8:1-3; Philippians 3:6). He was zealous in his pursuit of perfection (3:6). But then he met Jesus and Saul/Paul became equally zealous (but now more knowledgeably so) for Christ (Acts 9:1–22). The former wayward zealot became a zealot of The Way (Philippians 3:7–14). Soon the former persecutor became the persecuted (Acts 9:23).

It seems that zealots often need something to shock

them to change. God knew what it would take to capture, change, and commission Paul. He was captured in a moment of time on a road to Damascus. He was changed over a period of time by means of years alone with God. He was molded for years in the often harsh but rewarding crucible of ministry. And he was commissioned by Christ Jesus Himself to bring the Gospel to the Gentiles, an enormous task which Paul accomplished with great zeal!

Paul went from a political zealot to one determined to know nothing except Christ crucified (1 Corinthians 2:2), from a violent persecutor (1 Timothy 1:13) to a patient persuader (1 Thessalonians 2:1–12). He never lost his zealous personality (e.g., Acts 23:3). In Acts 21:17-26 we find the apostle Paul zealous for the gospel to the Gentiles clashing with fellow Jewish Christians zealous for the law of Moses. Paul lamented the zeal gone awry of his Jewish brethren—"their zeal is not based on knowledge" (Romans 10:2)—zeal of the Judaizers to proselytize (Galatians 4:17–21), and his own zeal once wrongly directed to "the traditions of my fathers" (Galatians 1:14). But he commended zeal in loving one another (Romans 12:10–11), and zeal in generosity and service (2 Corinthians 8:22).

It is ironic that the primary way Jesus gets through to the passionate is through His Passion. And the primary way He gets through to the political is through miscarriages of justice. And the primary way Jesus gets through to the hardheaded is through suffering. And the primary way He gets through to the activist is through a more compelling cause.

That's what Jesus did with Saul/Paul of Tarsus. He tracked down Saul, who was en route to Damascus and instead of neutralizing him redirects his zeal to a heavenly cause.

WALK WITH JESUS

The Zealots embodied many commendable traits. We can expect that these would not be missed by Jesus. The Zealots were jealous for the honor of God, like their hero Phinehas. The Zealots were people of action, not just words. We know Jesus liked this trait (John 14:21). They were people of passion, not indifference, and Jesus liked this as well (see Revelation 3:14–22). They were people of principle, not just getting along. They were courageous and willing to sacrifice. Members of the Zealots knew what they believed and were willing to die for it. The Zealots were champions of freedom, particularly religious freedom. As the story of Masada tells us, the Zealots were a devout people. They were willing to accept countercultural status, standing out and standing up for their convictions. Jesus, being a subversive Himself, seems to have had a soft spot for fellow subversives.

Jesus made it clear that He favored activists over the passive. In His letter to the church of Ephesus He lamented the loss of their love (Revelation 2:5). And in the letter to the Laodicean church Jesus said that he prefers action—being either hot or cold (3:15)—to apathy and indifference. In my experience, those who are heartily antagonistic to the gospel are often far easier to reach, and have more hope, than the committed indifferent.

However, the Zealots got some things wrong. Their zeal was often misguided, misdirected, mistimed, mismanaged, misapplied, and misused. Sometimes they were zealous for the wrong things, like man-made traditions, fabricated fences, temporary gains, and political kingdoms. Sometimes their methods were erroneous. Sometimes they sacrificed ethics for the cause and were guilty of ends-justifies-the-means thinking. Zealots often became like the very people they most hate (e.g., the Hasmoneans).

Zealots can become so consumed by passion that they neglect principle. They can sometimes act without thinking things through adequately, thus often encountering unintended consequences. In their action they cause extensive collateral damage, leaving many shattered lives in their wake. For these reasons, they often do not accomplish the things they fight for. They do not straighten what is crooked.

The righteous indignation of zealots also easily degenerates into unrighteous wrath. They usurp the vengeance belonging to God alone. They take matters into their own hands and thereby become dirty themselves.

How might Jesus interact with zealots today? Here are a dozen questions He might ask:

- Has the level of emotion generated by politics ever surprised you? Scared you?
- Have you ever wondered why politics grips your emotions so deeply? Have you ever pondered what fuels your political passion?
- Has your political passion ever led you to say or do wrong things?
- Have you ever found yourself sacrificing civility and truth for a political position?
- Has your involvement in a political cause or endorsement of a political candidate ever deeply disillusioned you? What did you learn from this? How did you change as a result?
- Have you ever considered the comparative emotional pull of politics and Christ?
- What has your priority on politics done to your relationships? Your relationship with God?
- Have you ever written off people because they do not share your politics? Have you regretted your action?
- Have you ever found your political ideology to clash with Scripture? What have you done with the clash?

- What would it take to transfer your passion from the temporal to the eternal?
- How do you handle brothers and sisters in Christ who do not share your political passion?
- What eternal (or even temporal) good has your passion produced?

WORK FOR JESUS

How might I be more useful in representing Jesus to people I meet who are Zealot-like in background and outlook? Here are seven areas to consider as you interact with those passionate for a cause.

1. Making a Connection

Jesus' connection with the zealots—and the Zealots—was about as close and personal as possible. Jesus lived for three years in daily contact with at least two political zealots, Simon and Judas. Jesus died between two zealots on a cross that was intended for a third zealot. And the resurrected Jesus would personally challenge perhaps the greatest zealot the world has ever known, Paul the apostle. Zealots won't be won at a distance, through argumentation, in a sterile environment. The best way to connect with a zealot is life-on-life. Jesus was willing to invest this kind of time to channel the passion of political ideologues to kingdom priorities.

The phrase "reach across the aisle" probably originated at church, but now is used almost exclusively of politics. It means to initiate interaction with those who have an opposing political position. Jesus did this in dramatic fashion when He selected Matthew and Simon the Zealot to be among His disciples. Jesus did not let politics dominate His kingdom agenda nor polarize His followers. Many say America in the early twenty-first century is as polarized as it has ever been politically. Votes now are routinely along party lines. Once people's political views are made known, walls rise, as does emotion, and avoidance is almost inevitably the result. Few issues divide us as people as deeply or make us as intractable as politics.

However, Jesus has crossed the political divide. From the get-go Jesus mixed widely with people of different political persuasions. He hung out with Roman compromisers, capitulators, and collaborators as well as Roman haters. Additionally, Jesus didn't make many political statements or have obvious political sentiments. Maybe Jesus knew, as we don't, that some things cannot be straightened. Jesus would not let politics interfere with ministry. Jesus would not let the kingdom of this earth usurp the place of the kingdom of God.

2. The Tone of the Conversation

"Personal space" is a phrase we use to describe that physical bubble inside of which we feel psychologically uncomfortable. We can converse with others comfortably when they keep out of our personal space. Only through time and with trust will we allow certain people "up close and personal." Interestingly, the recorded conversations Jesus had with zealots were remarkably close. Simon and Judas became part of the daily rhythm of Jesus' life. And Paul insisted that he and Jesus had met. Someone has wryly advised, "Keep your friends close, and your enemies closer." Jesus kept zealots close, and some became His friends.

3. Finding Common Ground

So many facts about and facets of Jesus' life parallel those of the Zealots, that common ground was easy to find. Jesus began and ended His public ministry with His zeal on display in His "Father's house." His courage, passion, and unflagging zeal for true freedom and righteousness caught the Zealots' attention. Threats from political leaders didn't seem to phase Him. Ultimately Jesus was tried and executed by the Roman government for "insurrection." Though neither a political animal nor junkie, Jesus knew politics like no other. And so He was uniquely qualified to understand the political world, from the panorama of a king at his birth to questions about paying taxes to Rome.

4. Losing the Found

Zealots have a double spiritual danger to deal with. On the one hand, they pass all the tests of religious orthodoxy; on the other, they are rigorous in their religious practices. So they combine both right belief with dutiful behavior. This can lead to an air of religious superiority. Saul of Tarsus is indeed a perfect example of this phenomenon. God has quite a project on His capable hands to capture the heart of a zealot like Saul and turn him into the greatest missionary, Paul. How does Jesus get this amazing man who thinks he is "found" to realize he is lost? First, no doubt God had a hand in Saul's development as a strict Pharisee. Mysteriously, God must have allowed Saul's zeal to become rabid and toxic. Then God must have said, "Enough." Acts 9 tells the amazing story of Saul's conversion, how a man on a mission to kill Christians became a "chosen instrument" to bring Christianity to the Gentiles. Then God tutored Paul Himself for a number of years in obscurity. Few have ever been so broken as a man who once regarded himself as faultless before the law (Philippians 3:6), but then learned to see himself as the worst sinner that has ever lived (1 Timothy 1:15)! A transformation of epic proportions took place in the psyche of one of the world's greatest Christians.

Zealots also tend to be cocksure of their political beliefs; zealotry allows little room for compromise. They operate, for the most part, in a "my way or the highway" mode. I find it telling that Jesus forced the zealots with whom He interacted to wrestle with important ambiguities. He let Simon and Judas, two of the Twelve, wrestle with the ambiguities of His messiahship—political or priestly. One failed and one succeeded. He let Barabbas and the "thieves" on the cross wrestle with the ambiguities of justice and injustice. One failed, one succeeded, and one (Barabbas) we don't know. And He let Paul deal with the ambiguities of bringing the Gospel rooted in Judaism to the Gentiles. He succeeded with highest honors! One of the tasks of those who would minister to zealots in Christ's name is to sow seeds of doubt in the minds of the convinced. To "sow" means one must be active—a trait admired by the zealous. "Seeds" implies small things done repeatedly. And "doubt" is one of the great ways God gets through to the cocksure.

5. Surprisingly . . .

The very fact that Jesus dared to choose people of such polar opposite political views to join His community of disciples is surprising enough. Choosing Matthew and Simon the Zealot is akin to selecting a radical left communist and a radical right conservative. Certainly this arrangement is a recipe for community division, not unity. Few things tend to divide as radically as politics, and Jesus took a very bold—and brilliant—step in choosing such different political persuasions. If we let down our guard, and disregarded some of our prejudices, we might find, like Jesus, that people are more alike than we think even when their ideologies clash.

It also surprises me that the zealots we have identified spoke so seldom in the Scriptures. Apart from Paul, the zealots say hardly more than a sentence. In my experience, politically inclined people do not and seemingly cannot shut up. In numerous peaceful settings I have been in a political comment shatters the peace and introduces rancor. And once a political rabbit trail has been inserted into the conversation, you might as well quit hunting for the truth.

6. Slogans and Symbols

My favorite activity as a kindergartner, apart from recess, was Show-and-Tell. We would bring some special item from home and then tell the class what it was and why it was special to us. Jesus seems to have modified this just a bit for He practiced "Show, Don't Tell" with the zealots. The recorded words Jesus spoke directly to political zealots are very few indeed. However, the recorded deeds Jesus showed to political zealots are among the most poignant in the Bible. Jesus' words are few to Judas, He never speaks to Barabbas, and says less than ten words to the "thief" on the cross. Even when Jesus speaks to Saul, the words are initially very few. Why? Maybe it is because zealots are people of action, not words, who regard words alone as a cheap substitute for action. Maybe zealots are like good Missourians who live in the Show Me State. Maybe zealots are primarily "visual learners." Some spiritual profiles need to be convinced by displays of power (Gentiles), some with acceptance (secular Jews), some with love (Hillel), and some with truth (Shammai). Still others value discipline (Essenes). However, the Zealots seem to be most impressed —and thus open to change—by what they see. Jesus shows Simon the Zealot and Judas His life for three years. In His Passion Jesus shows Barabbas and the "thief" on the cross Himself. And Jesus shows Paul Himself in heaven. We most effectively minister to zealots with deeds not words, and with show not tell. They respect it.

We say, "Seeing is believing." Ironically, this statement is true particularly with zealots. As people of action, zealots must see in order to believe. What they see must be undeniably clear. Every one of the zealots mentioned above saw something that deeply affected them. Phinehas saw in-your-face rebellion. Simon saw Jesus in action 24/7 for three years. Judas, like Simon, saw Jesus every day, but unlike Simon also saw money signs. Barabbas saw an innocent man condemned to die and a guilty man set free. The "thieves" on the crosses saw how Jesus died. And Saul of Tarsus saw a bright light and then saw the Light of the World.

If among your family, friends, or workmates there are zealots whose passion, and constant conversation, is about politics, argument will likely not succeed. They need to see. But see what? They need to see your passion for the Word of God (incarnate and written), your stand for justice and truth, your willingness to suffer for your beliefs, your willingness to fight for the right, your courage, your concrete actions.

The worst thing we can do to a zealot is to neutralize his or her passion. Indeed he or she may need a time-out (like Moses in the desert of Midian and Paul in the Arabian desert) to reconsider and refocus. But they do not need to "drop out." Slowly and gently Jesus seemed to try to redirect the passion of the zealots to new kingdom priorities. We can try to lift the eyes of would-be Christ followers to higher and better ways.

7. Connecting with Jesus

The passion of the Christ was the main way Jesus sought to connect with the passionate. Politics never had a darker day than when Jesus was crucified. Injustice, power plays, bribe money, inflated egos, political compromise, and abhorrent violence all characterized the events of Good Friday. Nevertheless, that which most grips the heart and changes the focus of a passionate zealot is Christ's passion. Simon the Zealot walked with Jesus through His life, death, resurrection, ascension, and beyond. Judas missed Christ's passion because of his own funk. Barabbas and the thieves on the cross had front row seats at Jesus' passion. And Paul "resolved to know nothing while I was with you except Jesus Christ and him crucified" (1 Corinthians 2:2).

The president of the United States of America is commonly called the most powerful person in the world. People everywhere document and analyze his every word and deed. I have for years found myself troubled by this common description for our president. Yes, the office is very influential, but I do question the individual's real power. For when we call any political leader the most powerful in the world, we reveal something about our true values. Do we really believe that eternity is real and more important than this world? Do we really believe those who wield political power are more powerful than those who wield the "sword of the Spirit"? Do we really believe the kingdoms of this world are superior to "the kingdom of our Lord and of his Christ" (Revelation 11:15)? Do we most fear the life and death of the body or the soul (Matthew 10:28)?

It is an ironic twist that the birth story of baby Jesus begins (Luke 2:1) with Caesar Augustus, considered by many the greatest Roman emperor. Not a soul on earth would have known that the baby in the cattle trough was infinitely more powerful than the king on the throne. But the baby, devoid of political power, turned the world upside down (Acts 17:6) and opened wide the gates of heaven, while the august politician did neither!

Profile:
The Essenes

Cancelled checks will be to future historians and cultural anthropologists what the Dead Sea Scrolls are to us.

—BRENT STAPLES

9

JESUS *and the* SUPER SPIRITUAL

Pilgrims by the thousands came year after year in the fifth century; many still visit today. Eventually four basilicas with floor space of some 5,000 square meters (almost the size of the monstrous Hagia Sophia in Istanbul) were constructed. All of the magnificent buildings were built around a rock pillar more than fifty feet in height and about six feet in diameter.

I had the privilege of visiting Qalaat Samaan, this strange holy site that is built around the base of a pillar (now only about six feet high). Yes, all of the magnificent buildings, and the complex that supported them, were built around a pillar that for thirty-six years was the home of Saint Simeon the Stylite.

Simeon (ca. 386–459) was originally a shepherd who became a hermit monk. In his quest to avoid worldly defilement and draw closer to God, Simeon lived (and eventually died) alone atop a pillar. He would not allow women to come near his pole, not even his mother. As his austerities increased, so did the crowds seeking to see him, hear his wisdom, and receive his blessing. And pole-sitters (Stylites) became popular in many places of the world. All Simeon wanted, however, was to be alone with God!

Every religion includes a small group of unusually self-disciplined devotees who renounce worldliness, separate themselves, and pursue God at great personal cost. We label them with various names: *ascetics*, *mystics*, and *monastics*. Apart from their serious (and sometimes secretive) pursuit of God, they are generally characterized by a simple lifestyle, studiousness, self-discipline, shared possessions, submission to authority, separation from the world, and acts of service. The ascetic, mystic, monastic group in Jesus' day were called the Essenes.[1]

INTRODUCING
THE ESSENES

Holiness was a hallmark of Judaism from its inception. Holiness to God was reflected in the holy Sabbath (Genesis 2:3; Exodus 16:23; 20:8, 11). Israel was called to be a holy nation (Exodus 19:6; 22:31), the mountain where Moses received God's law was set apart as holy (Exodus 19:23), Israel was commanded by God to build a holy tabernacle and then a holy temple (Exodus 26 and Deuteronomy 12), the high priest was to wear garments that were holy to the Lord (Exodus 28), and because God was holy, His people were called to reflect His holiness (Exodus 19:6, 23; 22:31; Leviticus 11:44–45). Moreover, the highest holy day for the Jewish people was (and is) the Day of Atonement (Leviticus 16; 23:26–32; Numbers 29:7–11). Of all the feasts commanded by God, this is the only one that commands self-denial (Leviticus 23:29, 32). Dealing with sin and its penalty is no trifling matter, and fasting from food was required. Thus, at the core of Judaism was the recognition of holiness and set-apartness.

In Judaism, some individuals and groups were specially set apart for service to God. First there were the priests and Levites (Numbers 3) and various subdivisions thereof (e.g., Kohathites, Gershonites, and Merarites—Numbers 4). They were set apart to and for God because of their genealogy, and to serve in the God-ordained corporate worship of Israel. Others chose to consecrate themselves to God. Foremost among this group were the Nazirites (Numbers 6). They took special vows of separation to and for God which involved certain otherwise acceptable things from which they abstained (grape products, hair cutting, and dead bodies).

Although Judaism did not formally include monastic groups, there were those within Judaism who lived monk-like lives. The desert was often their habitat, solitude and silence were their companions, roughness and rigor were often their methods, and holiness to God was their goal. Following this framework we find Moses, Elijah, and John the Baptist.

During the intertestamental period (ca. 433–5 BC) the Essenes "officially" began. They sprouted their roots along with the Pharisees during the time of the Hasmoneans. Detesting the encroachments of Hellenism on Israel, the pious ones rose up in rebellion, fought for religious and political freedom, and succeeded in creating a window of Jewish independence. Nevertheless, this window soon became clouded by politics so much so that those who once fought against the Hellenists started promoting the very things they had fought against. The keepers of the temple, the Sadducees, became thoroughly Hellenized. Some of the pious ones, the Zealots, became thoroughly politicized. And the keepers of the synagogues, the Pharisees, became (according to the Essenes) compromised. Thus, a group of the pious decided to became thoroughly separated. This group became the Essenes. They eschewed the temple, regarding it and its keepers as entirely corrupt, politics as ineffective, and normal life as impure.

Due to their separation from politics and the major

institutions of Judaism, the Essenes did not figure prominently in the history of the time. Josephus, the great Jewish historian, does, however, give us many details about the beliefs and practices of the Essenes. And it is Josephus that writes of a certain Essene, Menahem, who predicted Herod's reign. This apparently caused the king to grant some special privileges to the sect, including being excluded from taking loyalty oaths.

Our knowledge of the Essenes exploded with the discovery of the Dead Sea Scrolls in 1948 and subsequent archaeological excavation of the Qumran Community. Apparently, some Essenes continued to live in towns all over Israel, but others established monastic-like communities in wilderness areas to get away from defiling influences. In these communities the Essenes lived simply and communally, conducted themselves with strict discipline, frequently cleansed themselves ritually (like priests), devoted themselves to the study and copying of the Scriptures, apocalyptically anticipated the coming of the Messiah for the "sons of light" (as opposed by the "sons of darkness"), and were apparently founded by a mysterious spiritual leader called the "Teacher of Righteousness."

Certainly the Essenes and Essene-like (and Essene liking) people were present, and perhaps prevalent, in Jesus' day. However, when the Romans responded with a vengeance to the Jewish Revolt (AD 66–73), the Essenes were snuffed out as well. Moreover, because of their preference for celibacy, the movement died out sometime in the second century.

TENDENCIES of
The Essenes

T*ruth:* The Old Testament Scriptures were the acknowledged source of the Essenes' truth. They diligently studied and copied the Scriptures. They also added writings outlining their unique vision of their history and expectations.[2]

E*conomics:* The Essenes were materially poor and communally rich. They pooled their resources for the common good and lived, by choice, simple lives. So, though they were poor economically, they were relatively secure because of their socialized lifestyle.

N*eighborhood:* The Essenes were close within their own community but kept arm's length from outsiders. Since they believed that civic life was corrupting and the temple and its keepers were defiled, many Essenes separated themselves into monastic communities where they had a strong sense of responsibility to each other and pursued purity.

D*evotion:* The ultimate goal of the spiritual life was holiness (Leviticus 11:44). The means to holiness was self-discipline and communal accountability. This holiness was expressed by the daily diligent pursuit of piety toward God, loyalty to the community, and righteousness and justice toward one's fellow man. And the reward for obedience was the hastening of the coming of the Messiah.

Everyman: The Essenes "assigned everything to fate." Thus they accepted their destiny and sought to live their lives according to God's will, recognizing that He, not they, was in control.

Nature of God: The Essenes emphasized the sovereignty and holiness of the one true God, which evoked obedience and purity from man.

Civics: The Essenes were largely apolitical, and mainly pacifistic. They enjoyed the favor of King Herod, but generally despised Roman rule. By and large, the Essenes avoided both the contemporary political and religious scenes in Jerusalem.

Immortality: The Essenes believed in the corruptibility of the body; the immortality of the soul; judgment, including rewards and punishments; the resurrection of the body; and eternal paradise.

Ethics: The foundation of the Essenes' ethics was the Scriptures and the rules of their community. Human beings were responsible to choose right and avoid wrong, but to do so for virtuous reasons (love of God, love of virtue, and love of man).

Summary: The Essenes devoted themselves to purity before God and one another. To live a holy life was its own reward, but also made an invaluable contribution to the nation and was pleasing to God.

WATCH JESUS

According to Josephus and Philo, the Essenes were a fairly large group in Israel at the time of Jesus, not much smaller than the number of official Pharisees. Nevertheless, though Jesus interacted with the Pharisees on scores of occasions in the Gospels, He never directly interacted with a "card-carrying" Essene. He did, however, interact with various individuals and groups that had potential ties with the Essenes or exhibited common traits of the Essenes.

How did Jesus interact with the Essene-like people in His day? Consider these six encounters.

Cleansing the Clean
(John the Baptist)

At the Qumran archaeological site museum, a short video describes the community where the Dead Sea Scrolls were found. In the presentation, the suggestion is floated that John the Baptist may have been an Essene. Whether John was an official Essene or not, he most certainly exhibited many of the characteristics of the Essenes. He was a man of monastic-like vows (specifically Nazirite vows; Luke 1:5–25). He dwelt in the Judean desert (Luke 3:2). He was a man of God's Word (Luke 3:1–20). He lived a simple life (Matthew 3:4; Mark 1:6). He was celibate.

John differed from the Essenes, however, in four notable ways. He did not, to our knowledge, live communally. He advocated baptism for repentance, not ritual cleansings (Matthew 3:1–12). He interacted with the religious and the irreligious, calling both to repentance. And as a forerunner, he identified Jesus as the Messiah, the "Lamb of God, who takes away the sin of the world" (John 1:29).

Jesus' initial interaction with John the Baptist, His relative (Luke 1:36), is as short as it is sweet. One day the One about whom John has been speaking shows up to be baptized (Matthew 3:13–17; Mark 1:9–11; Luke 3:21–22). Though John wants to pursue holiness, he knows he is sinful. And he feels unworthy. Jesus rightly counters that His baptism is part of the righteous path He will walk to bring righteousness to humanity. John defers to Jesus, as expected, and then John is able to witness a startling event as the Father, Son, and Holy Spirit converge in sound and light.

John is a man who openly acknowledges the sin in himself and others. But now for the first time John has touched (and baptized) One who is entirely clean and yet chooses to identify with the dirty. It must have made John think. When we watch Jesus at work with John, we start to see the extent of Jesus' self-emptying (Philippians 2:5–8).

Out Essene-ing the Essenes
(Satan)

Isn't it interesting that the only identifiable group in Israel with whom Jesus does not formally interact is the Essenes, and yet the first act of His public ministry is with the Essene-like John? Jesus' second act, entirely private, takes place within a stone's throw of the Essene community of Qumran. Almost everything the Essenes stood for and against are mentioned or alluded to in the account of Jesus' temptation in the Judean desert (Matthew 4:1–11; Mark 1:12–13; Luke 4:1–13). The parallels are certainly intentional. First, formidable fasting is involved—forty days, no less (perhaps an allusion to the wilderness wanderings). Second, Jesus highlights the superior food of God's Word (the work of the Qumran sect was to copy the Scriptures). Third, the juxtaposition of light and darkness is obvious, with Satan being the chief antagonist. Fourth, Jesus, like the Essenes, renounces the kingdoms of this world for the worship of God. Fifth, the Essene attributes of self-discipline, austerity, humility, and uncompromising devotion to God pulsate through everything Jesus does. Finally, Jesus, like the Essenes, renounces power, possessions, and pride to follow God.

Although Jesus' encounter with Satan is private, I wonder if word reached the Qumran community about the man in the desert near them who fasted for forty days while fighting the temptations of the Devil himself? Personally I can't imagine that it didn't. And when it did, I also suspect that they were impressed. Here was someone, in their neck of the desert, who out-disciplined them. I wonder if they took note of His name, His growing fame, His messianic claims, and what became of Him? If I was enamored with self-discipline and someone came along who made my mortifications seem like child's play, I would take notice. Perhaps part of the reason Jesus was led by the Spirit to this place to be tempted was to bear witness to the Essenes. When we watch Jesus at work near the Essenes we notice that He set a humanly impossible standard of self-denial and God-devotion.

Follow the Leader

(John the Baptist's Disciples)

It is a mark of greatness to be able to let go—joyfully. Good parents do this when they let their children leave the nest with wings. And great leaders do this when they let their protégés work effectively for another. John the Baptist demonstrates his greatness, and his humility, when he encourages some of his best disciples to follow Jesus (John 1:35–42). The two disciples of John the Baptist who follow Jesus are Andrew (v. 40) and (it is generally thought) John, the writer of the fourth Gospel. Andrew then "recruits" his brother Simon Peter, and John would have in all likelihood recruited his brother James. So, some of the most important people on whom the initial "weight" of Christianity would fall, were originally followers of John the "Essene."

Essenes take vows of submission and obedience to the authority structure of the community. It takes a big leader to direct "his" disciples to another Master, and it takes a big follower to gladly go. Disciples are those who follow a leader. And the new Leader, Jesus, doesn't ask His new recruits to sign a multipoint contract; He simply asks them to observe Him at work. When we watch Jesus at work with John the Baptist's disciples, we notice that He called them to "see" more than to submit.

Feasting and Fasting
(John's Disciples, Part 2)

One of the most common practices of the spiritually serious is fasting. Most world religions involve some kind of fasting. Thus Jesus' lack of emphasis on fasting arouses the curiosity of John the Baptist's disciples (Matthew 9:14–17; Mark 2:18–22; Luke 5:33–39). Jesus had just come from a party at Matthew's house when some followers of John the Baptist come to Him and ask why Jesus and His disciples didn't fast (and presumably feasted too much). They know that all Jews who are serious about God fast.[3] The Pharisees were known to fast twice weekly (Luke 18:12). *So what is Jesus doing?* they wonder.

Spiritually serious groups often believe that as the end of the age dawns, fasting should increase. However, Jesus does not seem to see it that way. Jesus responds to John's disciples by saying that fasting is not appropriate at a wedding (Matthew 9:15). They, of all people, should have picked up the fact that John is to Jesus as a best man is to the bridegroom. And if John is the best man, then John's followers are his attendants.

Generally, Jesus is not a fan of fasting, nor is the Old Testament. Jesus shows considerable fasting prowess in the desert tempted by the Devil (Matthew 4:1–11). Nevertheless, He does not command fasting of His followers (though He did not forbid it either). Generally, when Jesus speaks about fasting (which is infrequently), it is to criticize those who are fasting for show (cf. Matthew 6:16–18; Luke 18:12). Jesus issues warnings about fasting on several grounds: motivation, timing, meaning, and results. Religious austerities frequently do not accomplish their presumed goals. Moreover, those whose self-disciplines are "successful" often find self-righteousness creeping into their souls. When we watch Jesus at work with those who fixate on fasting, we notice that He normally issues more warnings than praise.

Essenish Community

(Jesus' Disciples)

There is a sense in which the disciples and Jesus are an Essene-like community. Though they do not formally take vows of "poverty, chastity, and obedience," they do leave all to follow Jesus and as such live lives of poverty, persecution, and privation for the purpose of holiness to Christ and His kingdom.

The comparisons and contrasts between Jesus and His community of disciples and the Qumran community are striking. Both communities practice water baptism, but one sees it as a means and the other as a result. Both communities pursue holiness, but Jesus instructs His disciples that holiness is attainable only through the Holy Spirit. Both communities advocate separation from the world, but Jesus instructs His disciples to pursue this while participating in the world (John 17). Both communities live simply, but Jesus occasionally splurges and commends this as God-honoring. Both communities seek to be clean before God, but Jesus cautions His disciples that such cleaning is not external but involves a heart change (Matthew 15:1–20). Both communities teach commitment, but Jesus personalizes that commitment by focusing it on Himself. Both communities value work, but Jesus teaches that "sitting at His feet" constituted particularly meaningful "work" (Luke 10:38–42). Both communities enjoy communal meals, but

Jesus elevates the communal meal to a sacrament.

Matthew 10 records Jesus sending out the Twelve on their first official "mission." In His instructions to the Twelve, Jesus touched on several common Essene themes. One, the focus is the kingdom of heaven. Two, travel light. Three, live communally. Four, be wary of established religion. Five, expect persecution. Six, rightly prioritize family ties. And seven, follow the "Teacher of Righteousness." When we watch Jesus at work with His disciples, we notice that He took some pages from the Essene playbook but gave them a brand-new flavor, balance, and emphasis.

Taken to the Cleaners
(The Pharisees' Cleansings)

We say that someone has been "taken to the cleaners" when they have been bilked out of money or defeated soundly. The Essenes are known for their emphasis on cleansing. In fact, a peculiar archaeological feature of Essene communities is the number of mikvahs (ritual baths) that have been uncovered. One of the issues raised by the Pharisees is Jesus and His disciples' lack of "appropriate" ceremonial cleanliness (Matthew 15:1–20; Mark 7:1–23). If the Pharisees have a problem with Jesus' lack of ritual cleansings, then the Essenes would be scandalized by this striking omission. Jesus forcefully confronts the Pharisees on their criticism of Him by pointing out that their cleansing traditions are subtly God-defying, loophole-riddled, Word of God–nullifying, superficial worship–promoting, and man-made. But the knock-out punch of His criticism of cleansing traditions concerns the source of uncleanness and the method of addressing it.

Jesus' words are stunning. Nothing outside a person— no place, no person, no sight, no smell, no taste, no touch, nothing heard—is able to make a person unclean. Furthermore, the body part that most needs cleansing is the heart, not the flesh, and the cleaning solution is God's Spirit not ritual baths. When we watch Jesus at work with the cleansing crowd, we notice that He spotted a very different source of "dirt" and sold a very different brand of "soap."

WALK WITH JESUS

Certainly Jesus found much to like about the Essenes. John the Baptist, an Essene-like individual, was Jesus' advance man, best man, and one of the greatest souls that ever lived. The traits of simplicity, obedience, poverty, and community all were embodied by Jesus and commended to His disciples. Certainly Jesus could have related to the "dark night of the soul" so common among mystics and monks today. Clearly, Jesus was a Man of the Word and of His word, like the Essenes. I am sure Jesus would have commended the Essenes' quest for purity—though He would have wanted to discuss the means. Jesus would admire their devotion to God; their love of community; their pursuit of spirituality.

However, the Essenes' spiritual profile also had some peculiar spiritual flaws—flaws hidden under thick layers of protection, including community accountability, demanded disciplines, and hard work. The Essenes sought to build a community that diminished temptation. However, frequently this only serves to drive temptation deeper into the soul. The Essenes tend to miss, or don't even know they're missing, the liberty of the Lord. There is always the temptation that the path will devolve into law rather than liberty. Superficial cleansing is another fatal flaw of the Essenes. A true knowledge of the human heart knows that a satisfactory cleansing of the soul is beyond human ability. And the Essenes did not seem to properly reckon with the inadequacies of self-discipline and the spiritual disciplines. Discipline can easily become an end rather than a means. In the quest for holiness, the simplicity of a love relationship may be lost.

Jesus would likely point out their imbalance of not being "in the world" (John 17). Jesus would disagree with them about defilement (Mark 7:1–23) because you can't get away from yourself. Jesus would point out, as Paul did, that asceticism does not accomplish what it is purported to do (Colossians 2:20–23). Purity and piety are worthy goals, but cannot be attained by the flesh, no matter how self-disciplined.

How might Jesus interact with Essene-like people today? What might He want to talk about with you if you have Essene-like qualities? Here are several questions He might ask:

- Think of the person you most admire for his or her "holiness." What is that person like?
- What makes you feel spiritually dirty? Clean?
- Since you value self-discipline, what do you honestly think when someone else's self-discipline vastly outstrips yours? Do you become jealous?
- Since you are probably acclaimed by many for your religious devotion, how often do you encounter things said about you that you know aren't true? What then do you do?
- For whom are you fasting? (cf. Matthew 6:16–18)
- How do you view fun?
- How do you handle it when your devotion to God is "rewarded" with adversity?
- Have you ever found self-discipline to be self-defeating? What are the benefits and dangers of the spiritual disciplines?
- What impurities do you notice in your heart?

- Have your rigors to be holy uncovered new layers of unholiness?
- Do you ever struggle with self-righteousness, or its first cousin, contempt?

WORK FOR JESUS

How would you deal with people whose piety is almost palpable, who have voluntarily given up a lot in their devotion to Christ, whose purity stands out in stark relief to the prevailing standards not only of the society but of the religious as well? How do you reach the super-religious? How do you interact with those who put the vast majority of us to shame for their devotion to God? How do you reach those who talk a lot about God and what He is up to and what He is saying to them? How do you improve on people who are known for their purity, their piety, their community, their poverty, their chastity, their obedience, their devotion to Scripture and prayer, their longing for the Teacher of Righteousness?

How might you be more useful in representing Jesus to people you meet who are Essene-like in background and outlook? Here are seven areas to consider as you interact with those who seem super spiritual and seek to honor God.

1. Making a Connection

Breaking into an Essene-like group may be impractical and impossible. Usually such groups are semiclosed to outsiders, particularly to those who don't go through proper channels or meticulously follow "the rules." To our knowledge, Jesus never entered an Essene community, and no Essene to our knowledge ever entered His. Jesus did share many Essene traits and interacted with some Essene-like people. So I suspect Jesus' main connection with Essene-like people was word-of-mouth. I can't imagine that the dinnertime conversation at the Essene communal meals did not mention the peasant rabbi from Galilee, who fasted forty days being tempted by the Devil, who John the Baptist considered vastly superior to himself, who lived like an earthy Essene, who the religious leaders in Jerusalem hated and ultimately killed . . . and who rose from the dead. Sometimes the best connection we can make is via a good reputation.

2. The Tone of the Conversation

There is no recorded conversation between Jesus and any known Essene. However, this is not as strange as it may seem. For those who are Essene-like do not waste words. Like Trappist monks who value contemplative silence and speak sparingly, Jesus' "conversation" with the Essenes emphasized the sound of silence. When Jesus interacted with Essene-like people, He let His life and love speak.

3. Finding Common Ground

Jesus found substantial common ground with the Essenes. He shared with them the austerities of the desert, the waters of baptism, the challenges of community, the freedoms of simplicity, the solitude of singleness, the ostracism of the religious. Like the Essenes, Jesus experienced the intimacy of the spiritual disciplines, spiritual battles, and the passionate pursuit of righteousness. On every conceivable level Jesus could relate, point by point, with the Essenes. And yet they never met. Sometimes we least connect with those who are most like us.

4. Losing the Found

Of all the groups in Judaism in Jesus' day, the Essenes may be the hardest, and the easiest, to get lost. I know this sounds like double-talk. However, often the line between getting it and not is very thin. Let me explain.

The more serious spiritual profiles present more serious spiritual challenges. The ascetic life can stimulate pride or it can cause deep introspection. The passionate pursuit of righteousness, an Essene hallmark, has some built-in, and generally unacknowledged, dangers (cf. Romans 10:1–4). The greatest danger is that the pursuit will "work"; that is, it will enable the devotee to achieve a measure of spiritual self-satisfaction that they have succeeded in pleasing God by their self-efforts. And the greatest gift of an ascetic life is that the "relentless pursuit of perfection" will fail and out of the ashes we will find the One "who is able to keep you from falling and to present you before his glorious presence without fault and with great joy" (Jude 24).

5. Surprisingly . . .

Two surprises come to mind from Jesus' "interaction" with the Essenes. One, I am surprised by how little interaction there was. Josephus tells us that though some Essenes lived in monastic communities in inhospitable places, others lived in the cities. He also tells us that the official Essenes were not that much fewer in number than the official Pharisees with whom Jesus had extensive interaction. Why the "no-contact rule"? Was Jesus not holy enough? Generally Jesus' contact with Essene-ish people in the Gospels is very positive. Maybe Jesus didn't personally interact with the Essenes because He was content to get the message of the Gospel to them by other means.

Two, it surprises me that Jesus, after His temptation by the Devil, modeled so little self-mortification. We are told that on occasion He prayed all night, ministered all day, and refused food and drink. However, generally Jesus seemed to treat His body well. He enjoyed good food, received ample rest, and never "beat His body into submission." Moreover, the Gospels frequently depict Him at dinner parties. If the denial of physical appetites is a major means to spiritual maturity Jesus did not seem to model it.

6. Slogans and Symbols

"Keeping your balance" seems to me to be one of the most difficult challenges of the spiritual life. Every spiritual profile has its peculiar emphases and specialties. And the Essenes of old and of today are known for many commendable traits. The great challenge, however, is for these emphases and specialties not to become imbalanced; when they are, serious unintended spiritual consequences occur. It is a formidable challenge to balance grace and truth, mercy and justice, working and waiting, matter and spirit, dignity and depravity, faith and works, head and heart, to name just a sampling. Essene-like people seem to specially struggle with the balances of the sovereignty of God and the responsibility of man, mortifying the flesh and indulging it, fun and fasting, solitude and social involvement, being in the world but not of it, being earthy and eternal, and being content with both poverty and riches. J. I. Packer said, "Balance is the secret of successful tight-rope walking. It is also the secret of successful Christian living."

Several years ago I was on a riverboat at a wedding celebration. A woman I hardly knew came up to me and said she had had a conversation with my son. During the conversation my son had said something that surprised her. He said, "I have never seen my dad cut loose." I was heartbroken. My children knew my sober side, my ability to work hard, my dedication and commitment to my work. And this is all well and good. But he hadn't seen the other side, the fun side, the lighter side, the partying side. Some may have taken this remark as a compliment of their "holiness." I didn't. There was an important balance of life that I had missed. By the way, that very night I went out with my son and sang karaoke!

7. Connecting with Jesus

What attribute or characteristic or identity trait would Jesus most want to communicate to an Essene—ancient and modern? I think Jesus—the emancipated emancipator—would most want an Essene to find freedom. Warren McWilliams writes, "Several years ago a writer said he put a paper clip on every page in the New Testament that dealt with freedom. Almost every page has a paper clip!"[4] Essenism has the pronounced potential of stifling legitimate freedom. Devotion can easily degenerate into devotions, disciplines into duties, and discipleship into a grind. Just as license is the enemy of some of the earlier spiritual profiles, legalism is the enemy of the latter ones. Jesus would want Essene-like people to wrestle with His complete fulfillment of the law and what His completed work has done.

The movie *Babette's Feast* depicts an Essene-ish setting with Essene-like characters who live an Essene-like life that they believe is proper and pleasing to God. They live simply, semicommunally, spiritually, silently, stoically, monastically, celibately, and unfortunately joylessly. Into the Essenish village comes Babette, who happens to be a renown French chef. For many years she silently serves two very Essene-ish spinsters. But then Babette wins a sizeable amount of money in a lottery and decides to "blow" it all on an elaborate feast for the village and a handful of outsiders.

While eating the feast, at first reluctantly, the participants come to life, color comes to their drab existence, they seem to enjoy themselves as they experience a Eucharistic meal. One of the outsiders, a general, makes the point, "Mercy and truth, my friends, have met together. Righteousness and bliss shall kiss one another." It is this balance between the ethereal and the earthy, between grace and truth, between the practical and the pleasurable that expresses the heart of Jesus—and His hope for the Essenes.

CONCLUSION

As we conclude this quick trek through the eight spiritual profiles with whom Jesus interacted, here are five lessons we can apply as we speak to people from each profile who need the Savior who understands each and every one.

First, all the spiritual profiles converge at the cross. We should not be surprised that Calvary, the focal point of the life of Jesus, is the one place where Jesus has interacted with all humanity at once. After all, He said, "When I am lifted up from the earth, [I] will draw all men to myself" (John 12:32).

Though most spiritual profiles were present at the cross, their responses to what they witnessed could not have been more different. Some of the Gentile soldiers were so hardened that they made sport of a dying man (Matthew 27:27–31). A Roman centurion, however, recognized in Jesus God's righteousness (Matthew 27:54;

Luke 23:47). We know there were some women named Mary, who had once been detached and disenfranchised, there near the cross. They, through their sobs of grief, saw God's forgiveness (Matthew 27:55–56; Mark 15:40–41). And though we have no record of an actual Samaritan who watched Jesus die, perhaps an African named Simon of Cyrene and his two sons represented them (Matthew 27:32; Mark 15:21).

The group best (or worst) represented at the cross was the Sadducees. They were, unfortunately, the main instigators of the push to get Jesus killed. At the time, they most certainly felt exonerated and relieved to get rid of Jesus. Nevertheless, the aftermath of Jesus' death most certainly must have shaken them to their spiritual core.

The Pharisees at the cross were divided as always. Two great Hillelites, Joseph of Arimathea (Matthew 27:57–60) and Nicodemus (John 19:38–42), risked their reputations to give Jesus a decent burial, while other Pharisees mocked Him (Matthew 27:41–43). And both the Zealots and the Essenes were represented at the cross: one Zealot cursed his way to hell, a second must have pondered deeply his good fortune on earth, and the third cruised into paradise with Jesus; while the apostle John, once a disciple of John the Essene-ish Baptist, was about to become the caretaker of Jesus' mother (John 19:26–27).

If ever there was a place where Jesus would wish to

interact with every spiritual profile, it is at the cross. Today He desires to interact with the modern counterpart to each of these spiritual profiles, to a point of entering into a personal relationship (Matthew 11:28–30).

Second, the Beatitudes provide a provocative parallel to each of the spiritual profiles. I have long regarded the Beatitudes (Matthew 5:3–12), part of Jesus' famous sermon on the Mount of Olives, as the Bible's best portrait of a follower of Jesus. During my examination of the spiritual profiles, however, I became aware that these eight pithy and powerful statements of Jesus' coincide with the eight spiritual profiles chronicled in this book. Christ's blessing of relationship with Him and His never-ending kingdom are available for each profile.

1. "Blessed are the poor in spirit." The Gentiles, who realized their lives were broken, epitomize the "poor in spirit" who populate the "kingdom of heaven."
2. "Blessed are those who mourn." Stunningly, tears of sorrow and reactions of remorse are mentioned in most of the accounts of the disenfranchised Jews. Their repentance was profound, as was their comfort. Such comfort awaits all detached peoples who cry out for the kingdom.
3. "Blessed are the meek." The Samaritans were probably the most insecure of the spiritual profiles, being

"mixed up" and ridiculed as they were. Nevertheless, the security of the meek (not weak) came to characterize this profile.

4. "Blessed are those who hunger and thirst for righteousness." How Jesus must have longed for the power-hungry Sadducees to develop an appetite for the spiritually fulfilling food of righteousness. Today He desires all the powerful, and materially successful to discover the more satisfying filling of their souls.

5. "Blessed are the merciful." Hillel Pharisees, known for their mercy, hopefully discovered how much of God's mercy they needed.

6. "Blessed are the pure in heart." Shammai and his followers, often cited by Jesus for their hypocrisy, needed above all a pure heart, resulting in a true glimpse of God.

7. "Blessed are the peacemakers." To the politicized zealots, who were willing to kill for freedom, Jesus would advise peacemaking, a far more heavenly passion. Peacemakers and peace seekers today must learn they can find true peace only by becoming "sons of God."

8. "Blessed are those who are persecuted because of righteousness." To the ascetic and separatistic Essenes who endured privation and persecution in

their pursuit of God, Jesus would advise them to reconsider their cause. All who seek peace must find the source of true peace (John 14:27; 16:33).

Third, the profiles of Jesus' day seem to be prototypical. A quick survey of some of the classical religions reveals similar spiritual profiles to the ones Jesus encountered in His day. For example, Judaism today is divided into a variety of sects including humanistic, reform, conservative, orthodox, ultraorthodox, zionist, and Kabbalah. Islam also has its divisions, including infidels, secular Muslims, Ahmadiyya, Wahhabi, Sunni, Shia, Nation of Islam, and Sufi. Could it be that there is more than meets the eye to the timing of Jesus' coming to this earth? Perhaps the spiritual profiles in place in His day represent a prototypical palette of religious expressions. And Jesus was able to connect with all of them—and is able to do the same today.

None of the spiritual profiles with whom Jesus interacted two thousand years ago got it right; they all had characteristic strengths and weaknesses. I am eager to see how people of various religious persuasions respond to the online spiritual profiles questionnaire. But I am even more interested to see what happens when they interact within their spiritual profile with Jesus!

Fourth, spiritual profiles innocently develop traditions that inevitably color the truth. Who can forget Tevye's classic line, "Without traditions, our lives would be as shaky as a fiddler on the roof."[1] Indeed, tradition does give a huge measure of comfort, community, continuity, humility, protection, and stability to our lives. Tradition is, therefore, both necessary and helpful. However, an overview of Jesus' interactions with the spiritual profiles reveals consistent clashes with many religious traditions. From the outset of His public ministry He disrupted temple rituals, debunked holy sites, challenged the validity of the oral law, interacted with the "unclean," violated Sabbath rules and regulations, refrained from fasting, disregarded cleansing traditions, and ignored political ideologies. Though Jesus faithfully participated in some synagogue traditions and was the grateful recipient of the revelation of the prophets, His general disregard for tradition was a potent recipe for extreme hatred.

Surveying Jesus' interactions with the eight spiritual profiles we noticed two things: (1) Jesus unquestioningly endorses the teaching of the Scriptures, and (2) He seldom endorses the religious traditions He encounters. Jesus seems to regard tradition as more spiritually dangerous than we commonly do. Tradition adds to God's truth (the essence of legalism) and sometimes subtracts from it (the essence of license). Tradition, though man-made, routinely became sacrosanct. Tradition blocked effective ministry, prejudiced perusal of the Scriptures, rendered a false sense of godliness, enabled one to mindlessly go through the motions of religion without a relationship with God, and caused people to attach their emotions to appearances rather than reality. Tradition became the standard by which people judged themselves and others, neutralized people's ability to discern, created all manner of conundrums, and blunted some of the mysteries of God.

I do not understand why a phenomenon so clearly communicated in the Gospels, namely the homicidal power of religious tradition, should so readily be copied by those who claim allegiance to Christ. In our warp-speed world, tradition develops in months rather than decades or centuries. I suspect that some of the most pernicious traditions today are rather recent. Tradition is far more dangerous than we think!

Fifth, "All spiritual profiles are equal, but some are more equal than others." With due apologies to George Orwell and his classic book *Animal Farm*, there is a measure of equality to every spiritual profile. Each one has strengths and weaknesses, fine points and flaws. However, the pros and cons are by no means equal. Some profiles are "more equal" than others. Here are two key observations. First, the spiritual profiles that have the least exposure to Jewish theology (Gentiles, disenfranchised Jews, and Samaritans) seem to be the most interested in Jesus and have the most profound understanding of Him. Right from the outset of

Jesus' life, it is the Gentile magi who seek the Messiah, and the Jewish Bible scholars who are indifferent (ignorant?) to the birth of the King. And at the end of Jesus' life it is the temple-keepers and Bible scholars who want Jesus dead, and the Zealot thief and the Roman centurion who see life in Him.

Similarly, I have been in many pastoral settings where the godliness of "ordinary" members of my congregation has put my devotion to shame. Moreover, I have come to see over the years that the insight of God's simple people often far exceeds the wisdom of the experts. Jesus, for one, was enormously impressed with the spiritual perception of the "simple" (Matthew 11:25–26; 13:11). Why is this so? Certainly the reasons are many, but surely among them is the tendency of the simple believer to carry less theological baggage, be less skilled in Scripture-twisting, more inclined to read the Scriptures normally, have more real-world experience to draw on, and have a more earthy perspective on life.

Second, a rough estimate of the number of encounters Jesus had with the various spiritual profiles looks like a bell-shaped curve with the profiles more in the middle (Samaritans, Sadducees, and Pharisees) receiving the most mention and those at the margins (Gentiles and Essenes) receiving the least. Jesus thus focused His ministry on the large number of Jews who were spiritually close, but so far away.

Jesus is the Man of all spiritual profiles, to all spiritual profiles, and for all spiritual profiles. He innately understands every profile, He can uncommonly connect with each profile, and He is able to uniquely fulfill the deepest needs and longings of each profile. He was and is the Great I Am! (Jesus' eight "I am" statements found in John speak to each of the profiles.)

As the Son of Adam (Luke 3:38) to the *Gentiles*, Jesus was one of us. He became flesh (John 1:14) and experienced every human emotion and temptation common to humanity (Matthew 4:1–11; Hebrews 2:18; 4:15). As a friend of the *disenfranchised* and the detached (Matthew 11:19), He knew what it was like to be kicked out of synagogues and regarded as spiritual scum. In Jesus the disenfranchised found a *good shepherd* who would give His life for God's wayward sheep (John 10:11, 14).

Jesus' questionable origins (John 9:29), "strange" spirituality, and outsider status enabled Him to identify with the *Samaritans*. Like them, Jesus was not understood, not recognized, and not received by the Jewish people (John 1:5, 10–11). As the world's most secure Person, He built bridges where others built barriers, and brought living water to thirsty souls. In Jesus the Samaritans found "water welling up to eternal life" (John 4:14) and the *bread of life* (John 6:35, 48).

Like the *Sadducees*, Jesus was at home in the temple and

all its trappings (Luke 2:49; John 2:16). After all, Jesus had a hand in the design of the priestly clothing, the architecture of the building, and the rhythms of the rituals. No one understood true worship better than the One who was one with God (John 10:30; 17:11, 22). Jesus longed for the Sadducees to find in Him the *resurrection and the life* (John 11:25).

Jesus' sacrificial love for humanity (John 15:13) connected well with the Pharisee followers of Hillel whose passion was for people. Jesus' oneness with God caused compassion to course through His being (Matthew 9:36; 14:14; 15:32; 20:34; Luke 15:20). He could speak uniquely to the Pharisees about the extent of God's love. And He wanted them to recognize that the only way their quest for love could produce good fruit was by attachment to the *true vine* (John 15:1–17) of God's love. As the embodiment of truth (John 1:14, 17; 3:21), He spoke the language of the Pharisee followers of *Shammai*. Jesus longed for the Pharisees to see that He is "the way and *the truth* and the life" (John 14:6, italics added).

Jesus' zeal for His Father's house (John 2:17) must have intrigued the *Zealots*. Jesus, like none other, could speak the language of those sold out to the cause of freedom (John 8:31–38). However, He longed for them to see that true freedom is not found in Abraham, but in the One who said, "before Abraham was born, *I am*" (John 8:58, italics added).

And as the unique sinless sacrifice, He understood instinctively and practically the Essenes' quest for holiness. He could speak the language of austerity and commitment, but also of extravagance and celebration. Jesus longed for ascetics who so sacrificially turned from darkness, to see Him as the *light of the world* (John 8:12; 9:5).

Our spiritual profiles may differ, but only One makes an eternal difference. I pray that you have met Him in the pages of this book.

NOTES

Introduction: A New Kind of Profiling
1. Accessed at http://transcripts.cnn.com/TRANSCRIPTS/0603/03/lol.03.html

Chapter 1: Jesus and the Unchurched
1. Philip Jenkins, *The Next Christendom* (New York: Oxford Univ. Press, 2002).
2. "Unchurched Population Nears 100 Million in the United States" 19 March 2007, http://www.barna.org/barna-update/article/12-faithspirituality/107-unchurched-population-nears-100-million-in-the-us.
3. The sources on the Gentiles in Jesus' day are vast and growing. The history of the Romans during the first century is an ever-expanding field of study. Obviously, the Old and New Testaments, the Apocrypha, and the Jewish rabbinical writings frequently reference the "Gentiles" (*goyim*). And the historians of the first century include Livy (59 BC–AD 17), Josephus (AD 37–ca. 100), Plutarch (AD ca. 46–120), Tacitus (AD c. 56–ca. 117), and Suetonius (AD c. 69/75–ca. 130).
4. God's plan for the nations is highlighted in many Old Testament passages, including Psalms 47:1, 8–9; 49:65, 67; 86:9; 96:3, 10; 98:2; 99:2; 105:1; 117:1.

5. Everett Ferguson argues, "If for Greece the measure of all things was man, for Rome the measure of all things was law. For the east the measure of all things was the king, and it will be seen that for the Jews the measure of all things was God." Everett Ferguson, *Backgrounds of Early Christianity* (Grand Rapids: Eerdmans, 2003), 21–22.

6. "Jews frequently insulted Gentiles by calling them 'dogs'—the wild, homeless scavengers that roamed freely in Palestine," notes Blomberg. "But the diminutive form [used by Jesus] (*kynarion* rather than *kyon*) suggests a more affectionate term for domestic pets, particularly since these dogs eat under the children's table." Craig Blomberg, *The New American Commentary*, vol. 22, *Matthew* (Nashville: Broadman, 1992), 244.

7. Between the guiless Gentiles and the diabolical Gentiles stands Pilate. When Jesus is facing the cross and Pilate is facing a crisis of conscience, Pilate personally acknowledges Jesus' innocence but judicially decrees a death sentence. He caves to political pressure during his encounter with Jesus and the crowd. When we watch Jesus at work with Pilate, we notice that even the proclaimer of the gospel could not change a hardened heart.

8. A short list includes Joshua, Deborah (Judges 4–5), Gideon (Judges 6–8), David, David's "mighty men" (2 Samuel 23), Naaman (2 Kings 5; Luke 4:27), Josiah (2 Kings 22–23; 2 Chronicles 34–35), and Cornelius (Acts 10).

9. Thus Jesus was unafraid of physical, ethnic, and gender "uncleanness"; see Blomberg, *Matthew*, 136.

10. These three slogans are used by Nescafé, Nike, and Xbox 360, respectively.

Chapter 2: Jesus and the Detached

1. Three other reasons for dechurching I have observed are: (1) parents focus on their children's activities as a substitute for involvement in a church (for these people their "church" becomes the sports moms

and dads, their "new community"); (2) workers focus on job success, necessitating rest and recreation on Sunday; and (3) a person feels embarrassed or excluded by some life event (eg., a divorce).

2. As of 2006, 7% of Israeli Jews defined themselves as Haredim; an additional 10% as "religious"; 14% as "religious-traditionalists"; 22% as "non-religious-traditionalists" (not strictly adhering to Jewish law or halakha); and 44% as "secular." From "Social Survey 2006," released by Israel's Central Bureau of Statistics (in Hebrew): as cited in "Religion in Israel," Wikipedia; http://en.wikipedia.org/wiki/Religion _in_Israel.

3. E. P. Sanders writes, "Were we to survey Palestinian religion in general we would also find pagans, concentrated in a few cities. We would not find atheists. Formal atheism—the denial of the existence of a higher power—was virtually unknown in antiquity. Certainly some people lived as if there were no God, but true atheism was either non-existent or negligible." E. P. Sanders, *Judaism: Practice and Belief* (London: SCM, 1992), 20.

4. In *Esther* of *The NIV Application Commentary*, Karen Jobes notes, "Unlike Daniel and his friends, Esther shows no concern for the dietary laws when she is taken into the court of a pagan king. Instead of protesting, she conceals her Jewish identity and plays to win the new-queen beauty contest. Esther loses her virginity in the bed of an uncircumcised Gentile to whom she is not married, and she pleases him in that one night better than all the other virgins in the harem. When Esther risks her life by going to the king, she does so only after Mordecai points out that she herself will not escape harm even if she refuses to act." Karen H. Jobes, *Esther, The NIV Application Commentary* (Grand Rapids: Zondervan, 1999), 20.

5. Merrian-Webster's New Collegiate Dictionary, 11th edition.

6. "The tax collector's booth where Jesus found Levi was probably a toll booth on the major international road that went west from Damascus through Capernaum to the Mediterranean coast and then south to Egypt"; *The NIV Study Bible*, (Grand Rapids: Zondervan, 2002), 1528.

7. "Such perfume was very costly. If she used nard, for example, the cost would be about 300 denarii a pound, an average person's annual wage! Such perfume, like myrrh, was used for burial or to purify priests (Ex. 30:25–30)." Darrell L. Bock, *Studying the Historical Jesus* (Grand Rapids: Baker, 2002,) 218.

8. Matthew 27:56, 61; 28:1; Mark 15:40, 47; 16:1, 9; Luke 24:10; John 19:25; 20:1, 11, 16, 18.

Chapter 3: Jesus and the Syncretists

1. The sources on the Samaritans include the familiar ones: The Old and New Testaments, the Apocryphal writings, and Josephus, the historian. The Jewish rabbinical writings also mention the Samaritans, as might be expected, in a negative manner. And to round out the ancient sources, the Samaritans themselves claim their Scriptures (the "Samaritan Pentateuch") to be the oldest and best copy of the Law of Moses.

2. *The Works of Josephus: Complete and Unabridged*, trans. William Whiston (Lynn, Mass.: Hendrickson, 1982), *Antiquities*, book 18, chapter 2.2.

3. *The Mishnah*, trans. Herbert Danby (Oxford: Oxford Univ. Press, 1992), Shebiith, 8:10, 49.

4. The Apocrapha, trans. Edgar J. Godspeed (New York: Vintage, 1959), The Wisdom of Sirach 50:25–26, 325.

5. Kenneth E. Bailey, *Through Peasant Eyes* (Grand Rapids, Eerdmans, 1980), 48.

6. John 7:1, 13, 19, 25, 30, 32, 44; 8:37, 40, 59.

7. "PARADE's survey reveals a nation looking heavenward—but with its feet firmly planted on the ground of modern life. Spiritually speaking, Americans are a very practical people, moderate and tolerant in ways that would have astonished our grandparents"; *Parade* (4 October 2009), 4.

8. See Romans 12:13; 1 Timothy 3:2; 5:10; Titus 1:8; Hebrews 13:1–2; 1 Peter 4:9; 3 John 5–8.

9. Stephen R. Covey, George Sweeting, and others.

Chapter 4: Jesus and the Traditionalists

1. Sources on the Sadducees: The life span of the Sadducees was short (about two hundred years), the sources of information on the Sadducees are few (about four), and the attitude toward the Sadducees in the extant material is decidedly negative. The Apocrypha (I Maccabees) tells of the historical context out of which the Sadducees emerged. The New Testament mentions the Sadducees by name about a dozen times, and their presence is inferred frequently with reference to the temple and the priests. The Jewish historian Flavius Josephus provides the major historical and cultural background for the Sadducees. And the rabbinic writings (particularly the Mishnah) mention some of their beliefs and practices.

2. *The Works of Josephus: Complete and Unabridged*, trans. William Whiston (Lynn, Massachusetts: Hendrickson Publishers, 1982), *Wars of the Jews*, book 2, chapter 8; 14, p. 478.

3. The Sadducees and elders actually assembled at Caiaphas' home to plot Jesus' execution (Matthew 26:1–5; Mark 14:1–2; Luke 22:1–2). Judas negotiated with the chief priests to sell out Jesus (Matthew 26:14–16; Mark 14:10–11; Luke 22:3–6). Jesus was betrayed by Judas and arrested by armed men sent by the chief priests and the elders (Matthew 26:47–56; Mark 14:43–50; Luke 22:47–53; John 18:1–11).

4. E. P. Sanders writes in *Judaism* (London: SCM Press, 1992), 492: "Few [of the aristocratic priests] were despised, more were accepted as leaders. In the entire history of Israel, the longest period of tranquility had been when the aristocratic priesthood governed Jerusalem, under the general overlordship of a remote empire (ca. 520–175 BCE)."

Chapter 5: Let's Meet the Pharisees

1. *The Mishnah*, trans. Herbert Danby (Oxford: Oxford Univ. Press, 1992), Aboth 1.1, 446.

2. *The Works of Josephus: Complete and Unabridged*, trans. William Whiston (Lynn, Mass.: Hendrickson, 1982), *Antiquities*, book 13, chapter 5.9; 274.

3. Ibid., chapter 15.5; 287.

4. Babylonian Talmud, ed. I. Epstein (London: Socino, 1938), vol. 1 *Shabbat*, trans. H. Freidman, 31a, 140.

5. "Women, slaves, and minors are exempt from [the law of] the *Sukkah*; but a minor that no more needs his mother must fulfil the law of the *Sukkah*. The daughter-in-law of Shammai the Elder once bore a child [during the Feast] and he broke away some of the roof-plaster and made a *Sukkah*-roofing over the bed for the sake of the child." *The Mishnah*, Danby, Sukkah 2.8, 175.

6. Ibid., Berakoth 1.3, 2.

7. Ibid., Gittin; 9.10, 321.

8. Ibid., Shebiith; 10.3, 51.

Chapter 6: Jesus and the Do Gooders

1. Babylonian Talmud, ed. I. Epstein (London: Socino, 1938), vol. 1, *Tractate Shabbath*, trans. H. Freidman, 31a, 140.

2. *War*, 2.166, as cited in E. P. Sanders, *Judaism* (London: SCM Press, 1992), 446.

3. Sanders, *Judaism*, 415–16.

4. This event is similar, yet likely different, from the event chronicled in Matthew 26:6–13; Mark 14:3–9; and John 12:1–8.

5. For example, *Hillel and Jesus*, ed. James H. Charlesworth and Loren Johns (Minneapolis: Fortress, 1997); Louis Goldberg, "Hillel and Jesus: Comparative Studies of Two Major Religious Leaders." *Journal of the Evangelical Theological Society* (1 March 2000); and the websites moshereiss@moshereiss.org. and theteachingsofjesus.blogspot.com/2006/09/jesus-was-rabbi-on-hillel-side.html.]

6. G. K. Chesterton, *The Secret of Father Brown* (House of Stratus, UK: 2002), 8.

Chapter 7: Jesus and the Truth Seekers

1. Allan Bloom, *The Closing of the American Mind* (New York: Simon & Schuster, 1987), 25.

2. *The Mishnah*, ed. Herbert Danby, (Oxford: Oxford Univ. Press, 1992), Aboth 1.15, 447.

3. Ibid., Aboth 5.17, 457–58.

4. Not included in this listing is the longest, hardest-hitting passage in the Gospels about the Pharisees, Matthew 23, in which Jesus explicitly mentions the Pharisees as the objects of a series of "woes." Though this text perhaps fits both schools of Pharisees, the "hypocrite" label is more readily attached to Shammai and company.

   Jesus exposed seven inconsistencies: (1) concern for doctrinal purity was not matched by a commitment to put doctrine into practice; (2) passion for evangelism and missions didn't square with the product being produced; (3) disdain for dishonesty masked the subtle ways that truth was being fudged; (4) scrupulous tithing so soothed the soul that more important priorities were "righteously" neglected; (5) moral conduct in public was not consistent with internal motivation; (6) outer and inner beauty were not equivalent; and (7) nostalgia for the "good old days" concealed naughtiness.

5. In chronological order, the seven Sabbath healings are John 5; Luke 4:31–37; Luke 4:38–44; Luke 6:6–11; John 9; Luke 13:10–17; Luke 14:1–6.

6. *The Mishnah*, ed. Herbert Danby, Shabbath 7.2, 106.

7. Some concluded he was indeed the prophet (cf. John 7:40) whom Moses spoke of in Deuteronomy 18:15.

8. An entire division of the Mishnah is devoted to "Cleannesses"; *The Mishna*, ed. Danby, "Tohoroth" (sixth division), 603–804.

Chapter 8: Jesus and the Passionate Ones

1. Our information about the Zealots/zealots is primarily derived from the Old Testament, the Apocrypha, the New Testament, Jewish historian Josephus (*War* 2.8.1 [118]; 4.3.1ff. [121ff.]; *Antiquities* 18.1.1 [4–10]; 1.6 [23–25]), Roman historians, and Jewish rabbinical writings.

2. Note: In this chapter I use the word "zealot" in two senses. When the word is not capitalized, it refers to those exhibiting the characteristics of a zealot, but not necessarily part of an official group or party. When *Zealot* is capitalized, it refers to those who seem to have been part of a more organized and defined movement.

3. For example, see Deuteronomy 29:20; 2 Kings 19:31; Isaiah 9:7; 26:11; 37:32; 42:13; 59:17; 63:15; Ezekiel 5:13; 36:5; 38:19; 39:25.

4. For example, see 2 Samuel 21:2; 1 Kings 19:10, 14; 2 Kings 10:16; Psalm 69:9; 119:139; Proverbs 23:17.

5. *The Works of Josephus: Complete and Unabridged*, trans. William Whiston. *Antiquities*, 18.1.6; 377.

6. Ibid,, *War of the Jews*, II.8.11, II.13.7, II.14.4, II.14.5.

7. The Babylonian Talmud, trans. I. Epstein, Mas Yomeh, 9b, 38–39.

8. Matthew 10:4; Mark 3:18; Luke 6:15; Acts 1:13.

9. For example: Ho Chi Minh (Vietnam) had a middle- to upper-class background; Mao Zedong (China) a middle class background; Che Guevara (Argentina) a high-class background; Fidel Castro (Cuba) grew up in a prosperous family; Kathy Boudin, the Weather Underground murderer, came from a wealthy background; Osama bin Laden's family was very rich; and Umar Farouk Abdulmutallab, who attempted to bring down a Northwest Airlines flight on Christmas Day 2009, came from considerable wealth.

Chapter 9: Jesus and the Super Spiritual

1. Sources on the Essenes: The Essenes are not mentioned by name in the Old or New Testaments. The bulk of our knowledge about the

Essenes comes from the Jewish historian Josephus (who wrote extensively about them) and Jewish philosopher Philo (20 BC–AD 50).

2. Beside the *Manual of Discipline*, other manuscripts apparently describe the life of Qumran community: the *Damascus Document*, the *Thanksgiving Psalms*, and the *War Scroll*. They tell about the community's origin and history, its rules of life, and expectations for the dawn of new age.

3. God had first commanded a fast on the Day of Atonement (Leviticus 16:31). Righteous Jews after the Babylonian Exile had prescribed four additional yearly fast days (Zechariah 7:5; 8:19).

4. Warren McWilliams, *Free in Christ* (Nashville: Broadman, 1984), 19.

Conclusion

1. *Fiddler on the Roof*, book by Joseph Stein.

ACKNOWLEDGMENTS

Solomon said, "Of making many books there is no end" (Ecclesiastes 12:12), but I would hasten to add, "Of making any book you need some friends." I have been invaluably aided in the writing of this book by many friends. The seminal ideas for *Spiritual Profiling* were incubated on Sunday evenings in the summer of 2008. The give-and-take, feedback, and encouragement of this class not only helped shape the book but also gave me a sense that it was valuable for a wider audience.

John Medvetz provided invaluable research, creative ideas, and theological insight on each of the spiritual profiles. My "brainstorming" group of Roy Collins, John Crisfield, Chuck Erickson, John Osborn, Brad Topoham, and Dave Wahl helped refine the concepts and make them more real-world. Kevan Davidson and John Weeks offered exceptional expertise in the development and administration of the spiritual profiling online assessment.

And this project would never have been launched or come to fruition without the interest and encouragement of Randall Payleitner and Jim Vincent at Moody Publishers.

Finally, my family—Carey, Nathan and LeBechi, Christina and Iain, Susanna, Priscilla and Brandon, and Seth—have blessed my life more than words can tell.